PENGUII

THE DREAM FOUNDER

Dhruv Nath is an angel investor and a director with Lead Angels Network. As part of this journey, he has invested in fifteen start-ups and has mentored over a hundred others. Earlier, he was a professor at MDI Gurgaon and a senior vice president at NIIT Ltd. He has been a consultant to the top management of Glaxo, Gillette, Nestlé, Indian Oil Corporation, Thermax, Bajaj Auto and Air India, among others, as well as to the prime minister of Namibia and the chief minister of Delhi. Dr Nath has a BTech in electrical engineering and a PhD in computer science, both from IIT Delhi. This is his fifth book. He has written three books for McGraw Hill Education, and his fourth, *Funding Your Start-Up: And Other Nightmares*, co-authored with Sushanto Mitra, has been published by Penguin Random House India. Dr Nath is active on LinkedIn, and his posts can be viewed at www.linkedin.com/in/dhruvnathprof.

THE
DREAM
FOUNDER

*CREATING A SUCCESSFUL
START—UP*

DHRUV NATH

BUSINESS

An imprint of Penguin Random House

PENGUIN BUSINESS

USA | Canada | UK | Ireland | Australia
New Zealand | India | South Africa | China

Penguin Business is part of the Penguin Random House group of companies
whose addresses can be found at global.penguinrandomhouse.com

Published by Penguin Random House India Pvt. Ltd
4th Floor, Capital Tower 1, MG Road,
Gurugram 122 002, Haryana, India

Penguin
Random House
India

First published in Penguin Business by Penguin Random House India 2022

Copyright © Dhruv Nath 2022
Foreword copyright © Deep Kalra 2022

All rights reserved

10 9 8 7 6 5 4 3 2 1

ISBN 9780143457121

Typeset in Adobe Garamond Pro by MAP Systems, Bengaluru, India
Printed at Thomson Press India Ltd, New Delhi

www.penguin.co.in

To our glorious country . . .
. . . the start-up capital of the world!

Contents

Section V
Making Opportunities out of Crises

Section VI
Before You Leave . . .

Foreword

Start-ups in India have been booming over the past few years—and this is likely to continue. Just look at the exponential growth we have in the number of unicorns in the country. In fact, most experts strongly believe that India's time has come, and start-ups will lead the way. Quite naturally, there has been an explosion in the number of founders and potential founders out there. And since you've picked up this book and are actually reading it, I assume you are one of them.

Now, in the several years I have spent since I started MakeMyTrip, each day has brought questions with it. What should our vision be? What's the business model that will enable us to achieve this vision? How do we get the right people on board, and how do we motivate them? How do we translate the business model into action? And, of course, how do we respond to tough situations and even crises? Ever since I started my journey as a founder, I have been grappling with questions such as these. And I'm sure you—as a budding founder—would have the same questions.

Believe me, it is extremely satisfying to be a founder, and to create and nurture your very own start-up. But it's not easy. It needs a lot of hard work, some luck, and of course, good guidance during your journey. And it is in this context that you'll find this book extremely useful. I have known the author, Dhruv Nath, for some years now, and I have been impressed with his clarity of thought and ability to put things across in simple terms.

I've seen this in his earlier book, *Funding Your Start-Up: And Other Nightmares*, which he had co-authored with Sushanto Mitra. And I can see it in the present book, *The DREAM Founder*.

I was particularly happy with the acronym 'DREAM' that Dhruv has created. I believe it covers all the critical issues that you, as a founder, need to address. You must have a dream. And that too, a big dream. After all, I'm sure you don't want to create a small, stagnant start-up. And then, you need to build the right team. You cannot possibly create a successful start-up on your own. You must have a team where each member shares in your dream and is happy to work towards it. Which actually means two things. First of all, you need to get the right people on board. And then you need to develop them, motivate them, energize them. In this context, one of the most critical things you need to avoid is what I call 'founderitis', a 'disease' where the founder believes he knows everything and keeps micromanaging what his team is doing. Please remember, once you've got good people, give them space. Let them make mistakes and develop in the process. Instead of trying to do everything, you must be the nucleus around which your people develop and contribute to their potential.

That brings me to the other critical trait of a DREAM Founder, namely, the right attitude. Trying to micromanage, not giving your people space and not empowering them is a terrible attitude. Give them a chance to make mistakes, help them to learn from these mistakes and grow. And there is more. Be resilient. You will face problems, you will have roadblocks on the way, but you cannot afford to give up. Just hang in there. Think long term. After all, building a successful business is not a 100-metre race. It's a marathon, and you must have the stamina of a marathon runner.

But there is still more to attitude than this. Remember, the world around you is constantly changing. The business environment is changing, technology is changing, government regulations are changing and new competitors are springing up. I strongly believe that every founder must have the flexibility to respond to these changes. Please don't have fixed ideas. You must have the humility to accept the fact that your ideas could be wrong, and you need to change your thinking. Keep your ear to the ground and pivot your business model if required. Be steadfast but not stubborn. Just look at the most successful founders around you. Jeff Bezos of Amazon started off by selling books. Today, he is into almost everything, including groceries. And he also provides web services! Or think of Steve Jobs of Apple. When he started, Apple was making personal computers. And today they make iPhones, iPads, iPods . . .

Conversely, look at Kodak—the erstwhile market leader in photo films. It did not see the writing on the wall when the world was becoming digital. It did not pivot, and today it is dead. Or Remington Rand, the well-known manufacturer of typewriters. The world moved on to PCs, but it did not. And the rest is history.

Of course, execution of your plans is critical. Plans are meaningless unless you action them. But as I've mentioned earlier please, please, keep your ear to the ground. Look at what's happening around you. In case you need to pivot, do it!

One final point. You are, of course, aware that you will have problems along the way. No—you'll have crises from time to time, such as the Covid crisis of 2020, or the global financial crisis of 2008. Or even demonetization, for businesses that depend on cash. Yes, you'll have crises where you'll start tearing your hair out, trying to figure out how to survive. I believe that a good founder is resilient in the face of such crises. But a true DREAM Founder is one who makes opportunities out of such crises. Where he pivots the business model and perhaps charts out a different direction. That is what truly separates the men from the boys (or the ladies from the girls).

By the way, there is something else that I really like about this book. You see, it helps you to learn from other start-ups. In fact, Dhruv has described several start-ups in this book—all in the form of interesting stories. And most importantly, it includes not only success stories but failures as well. Now that's really great, because no one talks about failures.

To summarize, any entrepreneur will find this book to be a wonderful guide for successfully starting and growing a start-up. Above all, it is light reading, peppered with Dhruv's trademark humour! I would strongly recommend that you read it and keep referring to it from time to time. Have fun reading it, and I'm sure you'll benefit from it.

All the best!

Deep Kalra,
founder and executive chairman,
MakeMyTrip.com

Section I

The DREAM Founder

1

Introduction

Welcome, dear reader. It's great to meet you. Let me start by sharing some of the headlines that have been hitting the media recently:

'India sees third-highest number of unicorns in 2021; Byju's most valuable: Hurun' (Anwesha Madhukalya, *BusinessToday.in*, 22 December 2021, https://www.businesstoday.in/latest/economy/story/india-sees-third-highest-number-of-unicorns-in-2021-byjus-most-valuable-hurun-316497-2021-12-22)

'2021 in review: Indian startups bag record $36 billion funds in 2021' (Sneha Shah, *ET tech*, 24 December 2021, https://economictimes.indiatimes.com/tech/startups/indian-startups-bag-record-36-billion-funds-in-2021/articleshow/88464088.cms)

'Flipkart valued at $37.6 billion in new $3.6 billion fundraise' (Manish Singh, *TechCrunch*, 12 July, 2021, https://techcrunch.om/2021/07/11/flipkart-valued-at-37-6-billion-in-new-3-6-billion-fundraise/)

'How startup ecosystem can help India become powerhouse of global economy' (Byju Raveendran, *Indian Express*, 18 August 2021, https://indianexpress.com/article/opinion/columns/how-startup-ecosysm-can-help-india-become-powerhouse-of-global-economy-7457018/)

And there are lots more like these. As you are aware, the Indian start-up world has been growing exponentially over the past few years. And the next few are likely to be even better. The opportunity out there is huge. Which is why more and more bright young people (and some not-so-young people) are jumping in and creating their own start-ups. And thanking God that they were born at just the right time to catch this boom!

And, of course, one of these bright young people is you. You want to create a start-up, don't you? Or have already created one?

Now, how did I guess that?

Simple. Otherwise, you wouldn't have spent 300-odd rupees on buying this book! Or even if you had got it free, you wouldn't have started reading it. Elementary, my dear reader!

Now, having taken this momentous decision, I'm sure you are tearing your hair out trying to figure out what to do and how to make a success out of your baby.

Welcome, my friend! Welcome to the gang of 'founders-who-are-trying-to-figure-out-what-to-do-and-are-therefore-frustrated-as-hell'. And, by the way, I have written this book just for people like you.

But first, let me give you a bit of background about myself. No—I don't mean when and where I was born, when I proudly graduated out of nappies, or how I celebrated my first birthday. While I'd love to talk about all that, it's quite irrelevant to the present discussion. What I want to share with you is something fascinating that happened around fifteen years ago. Because that's the time I became an angel investor as well as mentor to lots and lots of young founders. Now, I must tell you that I had a great time with all these founders. We would typically sit in the open-air canteen in the Management Development Institute (MDI) campus in Gurgaon, or in some café in Delhi, and I would try and answer their questions over tea and samosas. Sometimes, burgers as well. And these are some of the questions they used to ask:

> 'We cannot afford to spend money on marketing. But we need to grow. So, what should we do?'
>
> 'Will I be able to get funding?'
>
> 'How do I scale my start-up?'
>
> 'Do I need a co-founder?'
>
> 'How do we attract and retain good people?'
>
> 'We have spent a lot of money on Facebook advertising and are now out of funds. What should we do now?'
>
> 'We are burning 5 lakhs in cash every month. Is there a way to cut that down?'
>
> 'We launched our start-up several months ago. But sales have not been picking up. Can you help?'

And so on . . .

Now, over time, two very interesting thoughts struck me. First of all, I realized that I could mentor, at best, a couple of founders in a day (after all, there is a limit to the number of samosas and cups of tea I could have in a day, isn't it?). Unfortunately, therefore, because of the lack of time, I was forced to say no to several founders.

Secondly, I also realized that many of the questions these founders were asking me were common. I could be sitting with the founder of an e-commerce start-up, or an online education company, or even an agritech company, but most of them had similar issues. Most founders had questions about funding, about their business model, about building their teams, about marketing without spending too much, about managing in a crisis. Yes, there were some specific questions, but in many cases, the questions were similar, and my advice was similar . . .

And one fine day, over my umpteenth samosa, it hit me. What if I were to put down all this advice in the form of a book?

I could pick up the learnings from all these interactions and weave them into stories. That way, I'd be able to reach any founder who wanted my advice (and I do hope there are a few of them out there). Yes, that way, I would not need to say no to anyone.

I spoke to my young friend Radhika Marwah, the wonderful editor at Penguin Random House India, and she was equally delighted with the idea.

And that, my friend, is how this book was born!

One More Book on Start-Ups? Why?

Good question. There are several books on start-ups out there. Just get on to Amazon or Flipkart and you'll see lots of them. So, why did I write one more?

Well, for a start, most of the books in the market talk about American start-ups—the Facebooks, the WhatsApps, the Ubers and the Airbnbs of the world. But hang on—aren't you planning to create a start-up in India? In which case, you would want to learn from Indian start-ups, wouldn't you? Sure, you can learn from Airbnb and Uber and all the rest of them—and you should. But isn't it far more important to learn from companies in the Indian context? All of us are aware that the Indian environment is very different from what exists in the western world. Most western countries, such as the US, are developed. We are a developing country, which clearly means that both the opportunities and constraints will be different. Small-town and rural India—often called Bharat—offers a huge, untapped market, with no parallels in the West. Language is a major issue, with the future perhaps belonging to start-ups that cater to vernacular languages. I can go on and on, but I'm sure you get the idea. While you should learn from start-ups in the US, it's much more critical to learn from start-ups in India. And that's why this book is all about Indian start-ups. One of the few in this category.

Next, even if you were to look at the Indian books out there, all of them talk about huge success stories, such as Byju's, Flipkart, Paytm and Ola Cabs. Whose founders are spoken about in hushed whispers, even at paan shops. And, of course, in bars, with alcohol warming the insides. I'm sure you would want to learn from these phenomenally successful guys. But let me ask you a frank question. Can you really identify with such start-ups? These aren't start-ups any more. They are giants—in many cases, multinational giants. Who do you really identify with? The smaller guys, isn't it? Those fledgling start-ups which are just a few years old and are perhaps facing the same problems that you are. Wouldn't you also want to listen to the founders of these young start-ups? Of course you would!

So, which ones do we discuss in this book?

Aha, that's the best part. We discuss both. On the one hand, the book has stories about young start-ups which you can identify with. But it also has advice from the real giants in the business—the likes of Sanjeev Bikhchandani of Naukri.com, Deepinder Goyal of Zomato, Annurag Batra of *BW Businessworld* and Meena Ganesh of Portea Medical. And then, we also have a highly successful investor—Sushanto Mitra of Lead Angels. They have all been happy to share their gyan, which I've promptly included in this book. So, you are in the happy position of learning from both the big guns and the smaller guys. And that makes this book truly unique.

But it gets even more unique, so do read on. You see, you can get lots of write-ups about start-ups that succeeded. Stories about their founders are plastered all over the Internet, the TV, the papers and, in fact, on virtually all kinds of media, except possibly posters on public toilets (thank god!). But what about those that failed? Shouldn't you be learning from them as well? To take an analogy from the film industry, if you want to be an actor, it is good to learn from Amitabh Bachchan. But isn't it even more important to learn from those who came from their villages to try their luck and are still pottering around as extras in Bollywood? Or worse, those who got fed up and went back to their villages?

Agreed? So, how often have you read about failures? How often have you heard founders bragging, 'You know, I'm really proud of the fact that my start-up was a failure, and I'd be delighted to have this come out in print'? Never happens, does it? Obviously, no one talks about failures. These things are never written about, which means you don't learn from them.

And that, ladies and gentlemen, is where this book gets really exciting. As I mentioned earlier, I have spent several years with young founders, investing in their start-ups as well as mentoring many of them. There have been some really successful founders, but there has also been a fair share of failures. And I decided, in all my wisdom, to write about both the successful guys as well as the failures. Founders who were simply not able to build and grow their start-ups. And whose stories have remained under wraps and, therefore, unavailable to mankind. Of course, in some cases, liberal doses of alcohol—duly funded by me—had to be supplied to get these founders to open up.

And that, ladies and gentlemen, is what makes this book really, really unique!

Well, not quite. Actually, there *is* one other book that meets all the criteria I've mentioned so far. It talks about Indian cases. It picks up examples from the small guys, along with gyan from the big guns. And it talks about both successes and failures. The book is called *Funding Your Start-Up: And Other Nightmares*. By a strange coincidence, this other book has also been written by me—along with my good friend and co-author, Sushanto Mitra. And, by an even bigger coincidence, this other book has also been published by Penguin Random House India.

The difference, of course, is that the other book is on the highly specific subject of funding. Whereas the present one is on everything that a founder needs to focus on—from getting a co-founder to building the business model, recruiting and building the team, marketing, creating opportunities out of crises, and just about everything else the founder needs to be and do. In fact, for completeness, I have even included some aspects of funding in the present book. However, if you want more details about funding, approaching investors, making your pitch, term sheets, shareholder agreements, series A, B, C . . . G, H, etc., you'll have to pick up a copy of the other book. And thank you in advance for the additional royalty!

The DREAM Founder

So, let's get down to business. What kind of founder do you want to be? A DREAM Founder, isn't it? Well, that's exactly what this book will talk about—becoming a DREAM Founder. By following a few simple steps:

D: DREAM BIG
R: RIGHT TEAM
E: EXECUTION
A: ATTITUDE
M: MAKE OPPORTUNITIES out of CRISES

One last comment. I'm sure you'll agree with me that nothing is ever static. Things change. The environment changes, government rules change, customer behaviour changes, technology changes, new competitors come in. Even lifestyles change, as we have seen in the Covid pandemic. And when things change, what do you do as a founder? Do you happily continue doing what you were doing earlier? Of course not. As a DREAM Founder, you must be aware of these changes. And then you must adapt. Be flexible. Keep changing your business model, depending on what you see around you. We call this 'pivoting the business model'. In other words, as a DREAM Founder, you need to be flexible enough to adapt—to the environment, to competition, to customer needs, to government policy and to technology. No fixed ideas, please.

So, how do you become a DREAM Founder? Just follow the five steps I've listed. Simple, isn't it?

Well, as you can imagine, it's not so simple. Otherwise, you would probably have had DREAM Founders bumping into each other at every street corner!

But there are certain things that can help.

And one thing that should hopefully help is this book.

Before We Move Ahead . . .

Before we start, I must tell you two important things. When I started writing this book, I realized I could not possibly cover everything that you need to do as a founder. You see, that would have made it a series of volumes—*The DREAM Founder Volume I, The DREAM Founder Volume II* . . . perhaps all the way up to Volume XIV (whatever that means). And you, of course, would have had to buy all these volumes. Instead, I've done something smart. I've looked back at the many, many founders I have had the privilege to meet. And I've examined all the issues that came up in my discussions with them. As I've already mentioned, many of these issues and mistakes were common. And I decided, in my wisdom, to focus on these common issues in this book. Of course, I might have left out something important. Do let me know what it is, and I'll include it in my next book!

The other thing. In most of the success stories in this book, I have retained the original names of the founders as well as the start-ups. But when discussing failures, I have changed the names. Similarly, when I'm talking about people issues, I have changed the names once again. And I'm sure you'll understand why. After all, if you were to meet one of these guys on the road, I wouldn't want you to say, 'Oh, so you're the person who could not succeed. So sorry.' Or even, '*Woh dekho* (There he is),' said with the inevitable smirk. No, I couldn't possibly let that happen. Therefore, I have created a few fictional characters. The stories are real—very real. But the names of the founders, their companies and, sometimes the settings, are fictional.

Who are these fictional characters? Well, let me keep the suspense going. You'll meet them as you go through the book (I'm assuming, of course, that you do plan to read beyond this introductory chapter).

But there is one character who is definitely not fictional. And you will meet him repeatedly in this book. The bearded professor, angel investor and mentor, who will keep popping up from time to time. Who these young founders go to from time to time when they need advice—usually over a cup of coffee. This character is very much real, and I do hope you recognize him. If you don't, well, just turn to the last chapter of this book.

So, happy reading. I hope you have as much fun reading this book as I had writing it. And I hope it helps you in building your own start-up. You are, of course, most welcome to connect with me on LinkedIn at www.linkedin.com/in/dhruvnathprof. Or on email at dhruvn55@gmail.com. And like the bearded professor, I, too, would be delighted to meet you and listen to your story over coffee and pastries. Funded by me, of course.

And I might just include your story in my next book . . .

2

The DREAM Founders of iDream

My first story is about two young men with a dream—Puneet Goyal and Rohit Prakash. Both of them were from the same MBA batch at MDI in Gurgaon. And they were former students of mine. However, I cannot claim any credit for what these guys have done, except for one thing: I let them sleep peacefully in my classes. A state of nirvana, if you know what I mean. And that might have charged them up to do what they did . . .

Anyhow, these two friends were passionate about—not movies, not cricket, not even girls, but—learning. Specifically, children's learning. And that is why, after completing their MBA, each of them independently created a start-up in the area of school education. Since they were both working with schools, they remained in touch. And life carried on . . .

But one fine day, something changed. You see, Rohit had been working with private schools. But that day he had a chance to visit a government school, and the state of affairs there came as a shock to him. Lack of teachers, no furniture, students sitting on the ground . . . How could children learn in such an environment? He visited another government school, and the situation was no different. Visibly disturbed by now, he went home to think. And then decided to meet his old friend, Puneet.

By a strange coincidence, Puneet had had exactly the same experience. He had also been working with private schools and had been equally shocked when he visited a couple of government schools. Quite naturally, when the two friends met, they got into a lively discussion. How could children in these schools ever get a decent education? How could they prepare for life? Was there a solution? As you can imagine, the discussions went on into the wee hours of the morning . . .

When suddenly, it hit them both! Could they help these children prepare for life by giving them educational support? So that these children could get into colleges and professions that they might otherwise have missed out on? In other words, could they bring high-quality education to schoolkids who could not afford it? Not just in cities and towns, but even in villages? And still run a profitable business?

Now, if you had met Puneet and Rohit (and if you haven't, I would strongly suggest that you do), you would have realized that they had another trait in common. Both liked to DREAM BIG. Forty kids, two hundred kids, one or two schools—no way! They wanted to make a difference on a mass scale. Whatever they did, it had to impact millions—no, crores—of schoolgoing children. And that, quite naturally, meant extensive use of technology. In any case, they realized that unlike many adults, children were very comfortable with technology. The more they thought about it, the more they warmed to the theme. Yes, this was what they wanted to do in life. With excitement at a fever pitch by now, they took perhaps the biggest decision of their lives (apart from the decision to get married, of course). They decided to merge their individual start-ups and work towards their common dream. And they hit upon a most appropriate name for this new start-up. They called it iDream. Where they would use technology to prepare students for life. And this story, ladies and gentlemen, is about the DREAM Founders of iDream!

Execution of the Project

Very early on in this journey, our two friends realized that having a dream was not enough. They needed to get into EXECUTION mode. And one of the first steps, naturally, would be to BUILD their PRODUCT. So, they started making rounds of government schools to understand the current situation. And they found something very interesting. Wonder of wonders, many of these schools actually had a computer room stacked with computers! Impressed, they spoke to the teachers. And then the whole story came out. Most schools had got their computers from large companies, as part of the CSR or Corporate Social Responsibility scheme of the government of India. In case you are not familiar with this term, the government has passed a law where large, profitable companies are supposed to spend a certain percentage of their profits on socially-beneficial causes. These include helping poor schools, building toilets or spending on rural healthcare, among others. Now, one of the easiest ways for any company to meet its CSR commitment was to buy computers and donate them to a government school. And that's exactly what many did. Unfortunately, it wasn't easy to maintain these computers even though this was covered under the CSR scheme. Obvious, isn't it? It was too cumbersome to carry these computers back and forth from the school. And the other option—that of sending an engineer to the school—was not feasible either, because it involved travel to remote areas.

The result? Once a computer went down, well, it remained down. And therefore, our friends saw lots of white elephants in the form of computers, carefully covered in neat plastic covers, with perhaps the sole intention of gathering dust.

Was that a setback for our two friends? Absolutely not. Instead, they put on their thinking hats and tried to figure out a solution. Clearly, they could not use these computers, so what else could they use? And one day, while taking a shower,

Puneet had a brainwave. 'Why not use tablets?' he thought, 'Something like an iPad, but obviously a much cheaper version?' Happily, they were able to locate low-priced but rugged tablets. These tablets were running the Android operating system, which—for the nerdy reader—is what runs on your typical Samsung or LG smartphone. So, tablets it was. The friends decided to create a lab with tablets in each school—typically twenty tablets in a lab, although this number could vary. And, quite naturally, the lab was called 'TabLab from iDream'.

Having decided on the hardware, they now had to arrange for the educational content for these tablets. Content that would help young students learn science, maths, English, social studies or just about any subject they wished to learn. This could be in the form of pictures, videos, animated lessons or simply multiple-choice quizzes. But at this stage they came upon a very important problem, so please stop gazing around and pay attention. In most of north India, the medium of instruction was Hindi. But in other states, it was the local language—whether Telugu in Andhra Pradesh, Gujarati in Gujarat or Bengali in Bengal. And some schools also gave you the option of English as the medium of learning (yes, even I didn't know this). Now our young friends could easily have said, 'Only Hindi. Can't manage so many languages.' And that would have been that. But remember, these were DREAM Founders. Their dream was big. They had to cover the entire country, whether it was Ladakh, Assam or Goa. Or even the tiny island of Dooba Dooba in the Indian Ocean (assuming there is such a place). But how would they manage content in so many different languages? Tough question, wasn't it?

And so, our young friends went into a huddle over doodh jalebi (milk and jalebi for you poor uninitiated souls who have never had this phenomenal delicacy. You see, Puneet was crazy about doodh jalebi. Once, he and I tramped all over Shimla looking for a government school where these young men could create a TabLab. And believe me, he drove me mad asking for doodh jalebi every time we saw a halwai). Anyhow, to get back to our story, the two founders realized that developing content for all subjects across all classes, and that too in multiple languages, would be a humongous task. Which would involve a very large development team and therefore plenty of dollars to be spent—actually rupees, but 'dollars' sounds so much more impressive, doesn't it? And that would mean—yes, you've guessed it—an expensive system, far removed from the 'affordable' solution our friends were planning.

But that's when they had a second brainwave—triggered by another round of doodh jalebi, of course. For Hindi and English, they would develop the entire content on their own. But for the other languages, they decided to buy out existing content from other local developers. And so, two major projects were initiated, more or less running in parallel. First, our young men put together a team of schoolteachers as well as programmers to develop the content in Hindi and English. And secondly, they went all out to locate existing content in the other languages—subject to extremely stringent quality checks, of course.

Now, the smart reader would have realized that they needed one more critical piece of software. As I've told you, they were getting educational material from multiple sources—perhaps in different formats. They needed one single software platform on which all these would run. A platform that would be loaded on to each tablet and would provide the children with multilevel menus for the educational content. It would also help the teachers monitor what was happening. And in the future, when the company added other kinds of content, such as e-books, this platform would need to support the new content as well.

As you can imagine, this platform—which we call an LMS, or Learning Management System—was at the heart of their solution. And our founders developed this LMS. They also created an interesting name for the LMS, along with all the content that was available on it. They called it iPrep. In other words, preparing myself for life—'iPrep from iDream'. Great idea, wasn't it?

Now, if you are concentrating on what I've been saying, you would probably say, 'Great concept in theory. But there are at least three operational problems I can think of. First of all, government schools would not have access to the Internet. Or even if they did, it would be highly intermittent, with low bandwidth, and certainly not good enough for the children to download animations and videos! Especially with multiple children doing it in parallel.' And you're absolutely spot on. Internet access in such schools would either be non-existent or, at best, quite sporadic. But our friends had an answer. They decided to load the entire iPrep software—the learning content as well as the LMS—on to each tablet and store it there. So, there would be no dependence on the Internet at all. Voila!

'Okay', you might continue grudgingly, 'These guys had solved the first problem. But what about the second one? Many village schools would probably not have electricity for hours on end. How would these tablets get charged?' The last bit, of course, would be said with a bit of a smirk. And once again, you are right. In many such schools, the TabLab could not depend on access to power twenty-four hours a day. But hopefully, there would be power available at some time during the day—or night. At what time? God knows. Maybe not even god. However, our friends had figured out a solution. They designed a special cabinet that would house all the tablets in the TabLab after class. Importantly, when each tablet was placed in the cabinet, it fitted into a connector, which in turn was connected to the power supply. Whenever the school got two hours of power, the tablets would get charged. It did not matter whether this was in the dead of night, in the morning or evening. The next day, when school began, the cheerful tablets would be all charged up and waiting for the students to begin.

And now I can see you jumping up and down. Because you still have one more objection, 'What about maintenance of these tablets? Wouldn't they meet the same fate as the computers that had been bought with CSR funds, and were now quietly sitting under dust covers?'

Aha, my friend. Our young founders had anticipated even this objection. You see, tablets are small and can be carried around, unlike huge desktop computers. So, whenever a support person from iDream visited a school, he would carry with him a couple of spare tablets, with the entire iPrep software loaded on to it. If he found a tablet that wasn't working, well, he would simply replace it with the functional tablet that he had brought along, and take back the non-functional one. Any maintenance would be done by iDream, or perhaps the tablet manufacturer, at a central location. No maintenance on-site and, therefore, no need for maintenance engineers to travel across all schools. Agreed?

As you can see, the founders of iDream had already thought of all three objections you had raised, so you can stop gloating. In other words, iDream had worked out a method of successfully OPERATIONALIZING the TabLab, and that too in tough environments.

But there was still one problem—and not a small one at that. Our founders needed money, or funding, if you prefer the term. The obvious thought was to approach angel investors (I assume you know what these animals are, but for those who don't, chapter 17 provides you the knowledge you need). However, our friends had other ideas; in fact, a brilliant idea. Why not tap into CSR funding? If companies were willing to provide computers to schools as part of their CSR targets, why not tablets loaded with software? So, they fanned out and started meeting large, profitable companies. Fortunately, they were able to generate enough interest and one company, which we will call Foodindia (name changed), decided to try them out. Foodindia identified two government schools in villages outside Bhiwadi in Rajasthan, and were willing to pay for setting up TabLabs—costing a few lakhs—in each of these schools.

So, the TabLabs were set up and began functioning. And you should have seen the excitement level of the kids (I mean the schoolkids, not the founders). They had never seen anything like this. Suddenly the world of science came alive. Animated pulleys actually moved on the screen. See-saws see-sawed. Even lungs expanded and contracted when breathing in and out. And what about that horrible, boring subject—maths? Even that became more interesting with geometrical shapes all over the screen. The kids really enjoyed it. The software on the tablets also had some projects for the schoolkids to do, and they almost jumped over each other to do them. For instance, some kids had created a model of a pair of lungs that expanded and contracted when you blew air into it. Another group had created a model car out of a matchbox. What fun it was!

Of course, the positioning of the TabLab was very important. Nowhere did the founders tell the teachers that the TabLab was a replacement for them. That would have been quite disastrous. Instead, it was positioned as a support to them. Some teachers would teach a particular topic in class and then take the children to the TabLab to review it. At other times, when a teacher was absent, the students would simply be taken to the TabLab and left to their own devices, which they loved. One school had no science teacher for months, but that didn't prevent the students from learning science on their own—in the TabLab, of course. In fact, when I visited one of these schools, I discovered that several students would stay back after school to 'play' in the TabLab. *Entirely voluntarily.* Just imagine, when you were back in school, if anyone had asked you to stay back after school for an optional extra class, would you ever have agreed? Silly question, isn't it? But these kids were doing it voluntarily, and that was the charm of the TabLab. And, by the way, at the time of writing this book, iDream had set up several hundred TabLabs in government schools across the country—from Rajasthan to Himachal Pradesh, Uttar Pradesh, Gujarat and Andhra Pradesh.

So, our young founders had created the brilliant concept of a TabLab. And they could have sat back and retired peacefully. But, of course, they didn't. DREAM Founders don't, do they? Once they have achieved something, their dream only becomes bigger. And this is exactly what happened to Puneet and Rohit. They realized that they had a huge amount of educational content, as well as a great LMS to manage and monitor all the learning. Why restrict themselves to only tablets? Many government schools were creating what we call 'smart classrooms', with a large whiteboard or even a TV where the teacher could display any digital content to the entire class. Several state governments were pumping funds into these smart classrooms. So, why not offer their content and LMS to these schools? The more they thought about it, the more they warmed up to the idea.

And that's how the second major offering from iDream was born. Our founders partnered with hardware suppliers as well as system integrators who would bid for these smart school contracts (for the uninitiated—not for you—a system integrator is an organization that brings together all components of the solution and installs it at the customer's premises). These companies would provide the hardware for the smart classrooms, and iDream would provide the content as well the LMS. As you might expect, business boomed further because now it wasn't just TabLabs that were getting built. It was the iPrep software running in smart classrooms, with multiple partners to push sales. And by the way, our young founders extended the content beyond just curricular subjects, to things like health and hygiene. They even provided access to e-books. In other words, iDream had truly become 'All learning for all children'.

The Covid Crisis

But then, disaster struck the world. In the form of Covid. I don't need to tell you what it did to school education. Schools were closed and learning shifted to online mode. An absolute crisis for most businesses. And, of course, iDream was no different. But just look at what the founders did. They realized that schools were shut, but at the same time, learning had to continue. Where? At home, of course. And therefore, they started selling their tablets, loaded with the same iPrep software, to children at home as well. Not only that, they also realized that the software would work equally well on smartphones, which many families already had. So, they also made the entire content available on the Internet, which children could download and use on their smartphones. In other words, at least those children who had decent connectivity at home would be able to access the learning online. And—hold your breath—they also created an app for teachers, which they called iPrep Coach. So, students and teachers were connected as well!

Now I must pause for a bit, because I want you to think about what Puneet and Rohit had done. Earlier, they were purely into schools. But when the Covid crisis hit, they adapted. They were FLEXIBLE, as you can see. In fact, they went a step further—they actually MADE an OPPORTUNITY out of the CRISIS. Just look at what they had done. They already had TabLabs and smart classrooms in schools. Now they had also made the iPrep app available at home. And finally, they had created the iPrep Coach app for teachers. A complete, comprehensive learning environment for children, supported by their teachers. As you can see, their dream had just become bigger. Because now it was: 'All learning, for all children, accessible from anywhere!'

Yes sir, that was the dream of the young founders of iDream.

The DREAM Founders of iDream

Dear reader, by now I'm sure you would agree that Puneet and Rohit are DREAM Founders.

To start off, they had a huge DREAM, which they were truly passionate about. And then, of course, they built the RIGHT TEAM. For a start, they had each other—the co-founders, I mean. They had been friends from their MBA days. Both had the same dream. And they complemented each other perfectly. Where Puneet was the strategist, Rohit was great at operations. Where Puneet was wonderful at getting orders, Rohit was great at making sure they were implemented without a hitch.

But it wasn't just the two co-founders. Each member of the team was handpicked. And just to give you an example of what I mean, here is the story of Pawan. Pawan was one of the first to join iDream. His role was to work with Rohit to install the TabLab in each school, train the teachers and students, and then support them over time. I have seen him in action, and I must tell you, it was a treat to watch him. You see, he had this unique gift of being able to level with the schoolchildren—and it didn't matter whether they were in class two or class ten. With them, he wasn't an adult giving them instructions. No, he was a child playing with them. And you could see that he was enjoying himself. The kids, of course, just loved him— they called him Pawan Uncle. And what about the teachers? They loved him as well, especially the ladies. They kept gushing about 'Pawan ji'. In fact, I strongly suspect he received a few matrimonial proposals in the process, although this has never been verified 😊!

But this story is not just about Pawan. Or Saloni. Or Manoj. Or Prabhakar. Or the many other wonderful people that iDream was able to get on board. iDream had the knack of getting just the right people into their team. How? Let's hear Puneet out on the subject:

Right from the beginning of our venture, we were very clear that getting the right people was critical to our success. Yes, Rohit and I had a dream. But that was not enough. Each person joining us had to share in that dream. We wanted them to believe in what we were doing. Not just talk about it but actually believe in it. We wanted genuine, sincere people. And for this, we tried to find out what they had done in life, which could go far beyond their résumé. In fact, we had each applicant fill up a questionnaire, which we called, 'Share Your Life Journey', which really helped.

You see, we were not just running a business. We were actually creating a huge social impact by helping underprivileged children to learn. Therefore, anyone who had done any kind of social work in the past—even informally—would be a great fit for us. I would say that this was even more important than the skills this person possessed. Skills can be taught. We have often taken on great people, even if they did not possess the requisite skills, as long as they were genuine and their thinking was aligned with ours.

So that's how Puneet and Rohit got the right people on board. But hang on. That's only part of the story. As a DREAM Founder, you need to constantly develop these people into a happy, motivated bunch. That is what we call the RIGHT TEAM.

Let's listen to Rohit now:

Having got great people in place, we needed to motivate them. To make them feel a part of the organization. And one of the things that really worked, is that we have been a very open organization. All information is available to our people, no matter how junior they are. We also realized that each person had certain professional aspirations—whether it was career growth, learning or anything else. We actually sat down and drafted a 'learning path' for each team member to help him or her grow. This learning path would be implemented and reviewed on a regular basis. And therefore, our people knew that they would keep growing and learning, as long as they stayed with us.

Execution

And now for the next bit. You are aware that DREAM Founders cannot simply dream away—perhaps in a hammock on the beaches of the Maldives, with the mandatory can of beer perched on their respective tummies. They need to get into execution mode. Now, let me ask you a question: As a founder, what would you want your start-up to do? You would want it to make a huge impact on the market, wouldn't you? To put it differently, you would want to bomb the entire market. Right? And therefore, we use the BOMB approach to EXECUTION.

What's the BOMB approach?
Simple:
B: BUILD your PRODUCT
O: OPERATIONS
M: MARKETING
B: BUSINESS PLAN

As you can imagine, these are four critical pillars of EXECUTING your DREAM. Of course, there are other things you need to do, such as registering your company, finding office space, locating a courier service, engaging a security guard, etc., but these are mundane matters. Till date, no founder has asked me for advice on engaging security guards or locating a courier service. Therefore, I will not touch upon these. Instead, I'll focus on BOMB.

So, to get back to Puneet and Rohit, you can see how they 'BUILT their PRODUCT (the first 'B' in our BOMB approach). Of course, the hardware was bought from vendors. In any case, iDream was not a hardware company. Some of the learning software, specifically the content in non-Hindi languages, was also bought out. But this is the key—much of the learning software, as well as the LMS, was developed in-house. And this is extremely important, so please listen carefully. You see, every business must have an entry barrier, which prevents competitors from copying you and therefore entering your business. Or at least, makes it tougher for them to copy you (see chapter 13 for more details). Now, if your business is software-based, it is important that you own a large part of this software. If you simply use software that is freely available in the market, your competitors can do exactly the same, can't they? And that's why the founders of iDream decided to develop their own software.

Next, let's come to the 'O' in BOMB, namely OPERATIONS. You've just seen how your operations strategy can mean the difference between success and failure. First, you saw that these guys did not depend on the Internet—which is, at best, highly unreliable in village schools and, at worst, non-existent. Instead, they had all the software pre-loaded on to each tablet, thereby avoiding the unreliable Internet. Secondly, they did not depend on a twenty-four-hour electricity connection. Because they had designed a cabinet where the tablets would get charged whenever the school got electricity for a couple of hours. And finally, the problem of maintenance was solved by simply replacing non-functional tablets in the school and carrying out maintenance back at the iDream office. That's right, our DREAM Founders had figured out everything, and were good to go as far as operations were concerned.

And now for the 'M' in BOMB, namely MARKETING. Remember, these guys had two kinds of clients for their TabLabs.

Firstly, they had schools. As you can imagine, that was no issue at all. Government schools were falling over each other to bring in technology-based learning. After all, it was a huge benefit to both students and teachers, and it was free. No, that wasn't an issue at all. Marketing was required for the other client—the organization that would pay for the TabLab through its CSR funds. So, what did our founders do? Did they place full page ads in newspapers? Did they advertise on Facebook? Or Instagram? Of course not. You see, they realized that only large corporations had a mandate to spend CSR money. Within these large corporations, they looked for contacts—people that they knew. They met these people, proposed their solution to them, and many of them were happy to agree. So, there was no marketing spend—it was pure and simple one-on-one sales with the head of CSR in the companies they targeted.

Who did the selling? One of the founders, naturally! Which meant that they didn't even need to hire a sales executive. Very low-cost marketing, as you can see. Later on, of course, our founders tied up with partners—either hardware suppliers or system integrators—who were bidding for smart school contracts. Once again, very low-cost marketing.

And now for that extremely important trait that all DREAM Founders must have. Namely, the awareness of what's going on around them, and the willingness to be FLEXIBLE. These guys started off with schools. But when the Covid crisis hit, they pivoted the business to allow kids to access the content from their homes. Which is potentially a far bigger market. Yes sir, they had truly MADE an OPPORTUNITY out of the CRISIS!

By the way, if you are awake (I need to keep checking, you see?), you would have noticed that I've missed out a couple of things. Within the DREAM framework, I haven't yet spoken about the 'A' or ATTITUDE. And within BOMB, I haven't discussed the 'B', or BUSINESS PLAN either. That's not a mistake. Patience, my friend. Before the end of the book, I promise I'll cover both of these.

And finally, next time you visit my hometown, Shimla, I'm sure you'll walk down from the Ridge to Lakkar Bazaar. And when you do, don't forget to visit the Government Girls School over there, where I have personally sponsored the TabLab. And when you see young girls beaming as they come out of their classrooms, you would know the reason why. That's right, they would have watched their lessons come alive in the TabLab. And perhaps read a fascinating book, which they would otherwise not have had access to.

And if you were to follow them home, you might, of course, see them playing hopscotch or 'catching catching', or any of the other games that young girls play nowadays. But you might also see them glued to their father's smartphones, watching hearts beating or lungs breathing or pendulums swinging . . .

Yes, dear reader, you would see that life has changed for these youngsters.

Because finally, finally, learning had become fun!

3

The Fascinating Story of Instamojo

So, you've seen one set of DREAM Founders. Now for the next ones. Two young MBAs, Sampad Swain and Akash Gehani. After his MBA, Sampad had created a start-up which Akash had joined as co-founder. They had a lot of fun and, ultimately, the company was acquired. And then, of course, both went back to regular jobs. But somehow, corporate life was not too exciting. Too regular and no real challenges. No sir, it wasn't working out. And one day the two got together, '*Chal yaar, dobaara kuchh apna karte hain* (Come on, let's do something together once again).' They had worked together in the past and understood each other well, so it made sense to do something again. Therefore, the decision was taken.

The only question was, doing what? In other words, what kind of start-up would they create?

Dear reader, tell me when you need to think, what do you do? I mean really, really think? That's right, I knew you'd get it. And that's exactly what our young friends did—they started thinking and drinking alternately (alcohol really stimulates the grey cells, you see). And gradually, an idea began to emerge. This was the year 2012, and there was no UPI and no wallets. Even Paytm had barely started. On the other hand, there were lots of people offering great products and services online. For instance, there was the dietician offering the most magical weight-reducing package on earth. Now you can imagine what a great business this was. First of all, much of the Indian middle class is truly middle class. I am, of course, referring to their proud paunches that bob up and down. With the men desperate to reduce their waistlines from a mildly overweight 45 inches to an athletic, V-shaped 44.5 inches. And, of course, the ladies too. Now, here's the thing. This dietician was not providing all this wonderful gyan for charity. She was charging for it. But how? There were no real payment methods available for small businesses like hers.

And then there was that phenomenal online maths tutor, who would guarantee 40 per cent marks in your next exam or your money back. And the painter who fondly imagined he was the reincarnation of Leonardo da Vinci and was selling his paintings online. And the small-time travel agency which got you train or bus tickets. In fact, it didn't even have to be an online business. Even a housewife baking and selling yummy cakes at home needed a solution for collecting payments online. Yes, she could have got the cake delivered to the customer and taken those crisp currency notes on delivery. But what if the customer cancelled the order? No sir, she would need to collect her payment in advance. As did all the other small businesses.

And that's where Sampad and Akash decided to give all these guys a method of collecting money online. They created a payment gateway and called it Instamojo. An extremely apt name, because it instantly added mojo to the small merchant. Whenever a customer bought something, the merchant would provide him with a link to Instamojo. And the customer could pay using his credit or debit card, or even through online banking.

Now, I want to mention something important. The two founders were clear that providing methods of collecting payment was not the end. No sir, their DREAM was much bigger. The dream was to ultimately be a partner for all small businesses in India. Not just for payment, but for everything else that they needed. However, as you would agree, you cannot do everything at once (unless of course, your name happens to be Mukesh Ambani, or something similar. And if it does, you probably don't need to read this book). Therefore, for the moment, they focused on payments. The rest was a dream, but it could come later.

Also, remember that these young men were helping digital businesses. And that meant technology. So, what did they do? Obvious, isn't it? They caught hold of two other close friends, Harshad Sharma and Aditya Sengupta, both of whom were tech cats. And that was the founding team!

By the way, I got an interesting insight into the working of these co-founders when I spoke to Akash. Let's hear him out:

> All of us founders have always had strong opinions. And we are not afraid to disagree—at times, very strongly. However, the interesting part is that our dream, or vision for the company, is common. Absolutely no disagreement on that. In fact, if you speak to any one of us independently, you'll get the same view. And that has been one of our biggest strengths.

Dear reader, I'm sure you'll agree with that. Having co-founders who have different visions for the company is a recipe for disaster, isn't it? Anyhow, to get back to their dream, our founders gradually started working on increasing their support to small businesses. For a start, remember I had told you that some of their customers were dealing in physical and not digital products? For instance, ladies who baked scrumptious cakes and needed a method of collecting payments. Instamojo already had a solution for payment. But what about delivery? Who would deliver those cakes?

Aha! Given their dream of supporting small businesses in every way, Instamojo tied up with local logistics partners and started helping these ladies deliver their cakes as well. And not just cakes, it could be home-made food, biscuits, chocolates, crispy fried octopus legs, or just about anything else. Now can you see how these founders were inching their way towards their dream?

But there is more, so don't go away. Remember I had told you that these guys had started off with payment through credit and debit cards, as well as online banking? Now, over time, all those wonderful wallets came into being —Paytm, Mobikwik, Yono . . . the list was endless. And, of course, the other big breakthrough from India—UPI. Added to the list was Google Pay, PhonePe, BharatPe and all the rest. Yes sir, this was the age of online payment methods. And the moment any new payment option came up, our friends quickly integrated it with their gateway. And that's a lesson for you, dear reader. Grab opportunities fast. Be quick or you'll be left behind by your competitors.

Now, I'm sure you thought that was it. After all, Instamojo had already integrated every payment method worth its salt—and several that were probably not worth their salt—into its gateway. But no. In their keenness to grab more and more of the online payments market, banks started coming out with easy-to-pay EMI (equated monthly instalments) options using credit cards. And what did Instamojo do? I don't need to tell you, do I? That's right, EMIs were promptly integrated into the Instamojo gateway. And since these guys are DREAM Founders, if any new payment mechanism is launched in future, they will make it available pronto. And oh, I forgot to mention, if the small business needed a short-term loan to take care of working capital, even that was provided. By Instamojo, of course, which had tied up with non-banking finance companies (NBFCs)!

By the way, there are a couple of other things I must tell you about these founders. They were very choosy about the people they selected. And having got these people on board, they would build them into a high-performing team. In Akash's own words:

> Right from the beginning, we realized that people were our biggest asset. As founders, we have always been extremely selective

about the people we take on board. Sometimes, we got great people with just the right skills and experience, but the vibes were not right. For instance, someone who was not likely to be a team player, and therefore would mess up the culture in the organization. In such cases, we would simply reject the guy. And in case we did make a mistake—after all, we were human—we would part ways sooner rather than later. Too bad if the person was good at his job. Conversely, if we got a great person who we wanted to take, but we didn't have a role for him, guess what? We would create a role for him!

Having taken on these people, we provided them with an environment where they could flourish. Lots and lots of communication about our vision and what we were trying to do. Lots of town halls. In fact, Instamojo has always been a very open organization. To the extent that much of our MIS (management information system), which talks about our business numbers, has been freely accessible to everyone. And our people are given freedom to express themselves, even if it is to criticize the working of the organization. In our earlier days, all of us used to have lunch together, and usually put on a movie or a stand-up comedy show while we ate. I strongly believe that getting the right people on board and getting them to feel that they belong, motivates them to perform!

And what was the result of all this? Terrific, as you might imagine! Instamojo was able to grow more than 100 per cent year-on-year. These young men had truly created a market leader in their chosen space—that of payment systems for small digital businesses. Yes, in their attempt to grow rapidly, they were burning cash, but they continued to get funding. And things were hunky dory . . .

Well, not quite. Around the year 2017 they faced a crisis. Yes sir, a real crisis. Our founders were looking for funding to sustain their continuous growth. But for once, the funding did not come. Why? Perhaps there were too many companies in the payments space—the likes of Razorpay and PayU—all competing for the same funds. Whatever the reason, Instamojo was left with no funds and almost no runway. And just for those who don't understand this simple fact, they did not have enough money to last more than perhaps a couple of months. Period.

Now there is a hackneyed saying, 'When the going gets tough, the tough get going.' Instead of sitting back and cribbing, our young men decided to fight it out. And there were two major steps in the fight. First, they had to cut costs so as to make the business sustainable even without funds. And that's exactly what they did. They cut unnecessary costs ruthlessly. For instance, one of their major components of cost was the monthly spend on lots of software products. They took a close look at each one of these and either dropped it or switched to a cheaper one. Even a free version in some cases.

Marketing spend was cut down to zero. Yes, zero. And the interesting thing our young founders discovered, was that their business could actually grow significantly, even without spending on marketing. Why? It's actually quite simple. Let's take the example of the wonderful online dietician we spoke about a few pages ago. She would be using Instamojo to collect payments. And she would obviously have customers—fat ones. Some of whom would themselves be small businesspeople who wanted to go digital, and would therefore need a method of collecting payments online. And if their experience with Instamojo was great—which it was—well, they would sign up as well. You see? Our founders realized that this method of marketing, where they spent absolutely nothing, worked brilliantly. By the way, we call this 'viral marketing', where the word spreads like a virus without the company having to spend. As you can imagine, Instamojo was able to last out this tough period. Wonder of wonders, they continued to grow during this time even without any marketing spend. Not only that, because of the cost-cutting, the company also became profitable. And the icing on the cake? Investors started showing interest once again.

But our young friends realized that they could not afford to go through yet another crisis of this kind. And so they went back to their dream. Remember, I had told you that they wanted to support small online businesses in all respects? So far, they had provided them with methods of collecting payment and were also helping them with deliveries. But the cash flow crisis had made them realize something. They realized that the time had come to take the second major step towards achieving their dream. The dream of helping these businesses create a full-fledged e-commerce venture. In other words, an online storefront.

Now, it is important to understand how these young men pivoted. You see, they had two options. The first option was to build this kind of storefront from scratch. But that would have taken time. And in the digital world, my friend, time is the one thing you do not have. A far better option was to scout around and buy out an existing player in that space. And after hunting around, they finally decided to acquire another start-up called GetMeAShop. Which was in the business of providing simple, affordable storefronts for small businesses. The best part was that by now investors had realized that these guys were fighters. They were making an opportunity out of the crisis they faced. And they were willing to fund the company once again—so money was no longer an issue.

Once the acquisition was done, Instamojo's customers could let *their customers* shop online, in addition to accepting payments online, all through Instamojo. In fact, the company's focus is now e-commerce for small businesses, and providing payment solutions is simply a part of it. Which gives the company far more scope for growth. As you can imagine, business is booming once again, and Instamojo is now a clear market leader in the space. Wasn't that a wonderful implementation of the dream of our founders?

Today, these young men as well as their investors are gung-ho about the future. And now a message for you, dear founder. If you want to launch a small online business today, look no further than Instamojo. They have helped thousands of people like you to grow their business. And they will help you as well. And there is one thing I can tell you with confidence. The day is not far off when India will see another unicorn. A unicorn called Instamojo . . .

The DREAM Founders of Instamojo

I probably don't need to write this bit, do I? Isn't it obvious? Four founders, all with a shared DREAM. And the dream was nothing if not big. In fact, it was huge—and they built just the RIGHT TEAM to realize this dream. Because all of them had an obsession about taking on just the right people (remember Akash's comment where he clearly said that even competent people would not be selected if the vibes were not OK?). And then, of course, they did whatever they could to motivate and develop them. Through an open environment, through sharing and, ultimately, through building up a large, happy family.

One interesting comment: Have you noticed how both Instamojo and iDream had a similar approach to building their teams? That's right, if you want to build a solid, growing start-up, this is just the kind of environment you need to create for your team.

And what about EXECUTION? Well, let's go right back to the BOMB approach we saw with iDream. First, take a look at how they BUILT their PRODUCT. They kept their eyes and ears open for any new payment mechanism that the country would throw at them. And they would immediately integrate it into their offering. Yes, my friend, once you have developed your product, you cannot sit back and relax in the Himalayas (or even in Switzerland if you happen to have a rich father). Because the world around you will keep changing, your competitors will keep adapting, and if you don't—well, you'll be left far behind! So, building your product is not a one-time activity. It's an ongoing process.

But look at what happened later. When the founders decided to move whole hog into e-commerce. They had the option of building this product on their own, but instead they decided to buy out an entire company, GetMeAShop. Why? Because it was much faster to buy out an existing, proven product, rather than building it from scratch. And these are decisions that you will need to take from time to time.

I also want to talk about their approach to MARKETING. Specifically, their focus on low-cost marketing. Remember, these guys managed to survive and even grow with very little marketing spend. Why? Three reasons. First, they focused on a strong social media presence, which pushed up awareness of the brand and the offering at virtually no cost. Secondly, equal focus on search engine optimization (SEO), which again was virtually zero cost marketing. Incidentally, both these approaches helped the founders to overcome the crisis in 2017, when they did not have money. And, of course, the virality in the business, where the customer's customer used their payment mechanism, and in many cases also became a customer herself.

And finally, when our founders faced a crisis, they were FLEXIBLE enough to pivot the business model and MAKE an OPPORTUNITY out of the CRISIS.

Yes sir, these guys are truly DREAM Founders. Why else do you think I've included their story in this book?

Let's Meet Sanjeev Bikhchandani, founder and vice chairman, Naukri.com

Who hasn't heard of Sanjeev Bikhchandani? The phenomenally successful founder and vice chairman of Info Edge, the company that owns market-leading Internet giants like Naukri.com, JeevanSaathi.com and 99acres.com. Not only that, his company has also invested in other market leaders like Zomato and Policybazaar.com. That's right, Sanjeev is among the topmost founders in the Internet space in India. A true DREAM Founder, with over two decades of experience. As you can imagine, he has a phenomenal amount of wisdom to share with all of you founders, and he is always willing to share his thoughts. I requested Sanjeev to share his vision of a DREAM Founder with you, and he readily agreed. This is what he had to say:

One of the most important traits that a founder must have, is customer orientation. Be close to your customer. Understand his or her needs. Figure out the customer's pain points. Get constant feedback from your customer. Remember, the customer is the one who brings in the money. Without the customer, you don't have a business.

The second major issue is a statement from the famous Hindi movie, *Deewaar*: Be a '*lambi race ka ghoda*. (in simple terms—as a founder you must be in the game for the long run)'. Not one year, not two years. Definitely not, 'Let me try this for a couple of years, otherwise I'll take up a job.' No way. Building a great company is the commitment of a lifetime. Yes, you'll have all kinds of problems along the way, but you've got to keep at it. Persevere, and you'll be able to build your company.

The third key trait is that you've got to be a personal magnet for talent. People don't work for companies—they work for people. They work for people who give them a fair deal. They look for bosses who are more than willing to take the blame for something that goes wrong, but share the credit for what goes right. They look for founders who 'Eat Last'. In very simple terms, you are the founder, and therefore you have a large stake in your company. Your team does not. Therefore, you must be prepared to give your stars a bigger salary than you yourself take. In a crisis, you should be the first to take a salary cut. These are some of the things that earn you respect and trust. And make people want to work for you.

By the way, this issue of treating people fairly and building trust, does not apply to employees alone. It applies to anyone you are dealing with—whether it is customers, or partners, or investors. Treat people and their money and time with respect. Be personally frugal. Remember, you have taken money from investors, and the last thing they want is for you to spend it on a fancy car, or business class travel, or a plush office. Even if you haven't been funded, you need to create a viable business—and big-time spending on unnecessary things will not help. Please remember, you are the role model for your entire team. If they see you splurging, how do you think they will conduct themselves? So, if you expect your colleagues to travel economy class and share rooms in a three-star hotel, be prepared to do the same yourself.

Of course, you've got to be a great salesperson. Don't leave it just to your managers. As the founder of the company, you are the chief salesperson. And what if you have never sold before? Well, start selling. Learn. In fact, I'll take it a step further. A DREAM Founder must have the ability to think both big and small at the same time. Big, because that's your DREAM, your vision. And small, because you should be willing to get into details and execute your plans. Be willing to do anything. Get your hands dirty. As a founder, you cannot sit in an ivory tower and say, 'This is not my job.'

And finally, you must be ethical in all your dealings. Corporate governance and transparency are critical to the success of your business. No hanky-panky. People—whether it is employees, or partners, or customers, or just about anyone else—must have confidence that they are dealing with a clean, ethical company. A company and a founder that they can trust.

Remember, in the final analysis, your only asset is your reputation!

Brilliantly put, Sanjeev. All the founders reading this book will be thanking you and following your advice. Thanks ever so much.

4

The Perfect Attitude

And now for the one thing I haven't spoken about so far. One of the most crucial bits in becoming a DREAM Founder, namely ATTITUDE. As you can imagine, attitude is not very easy to describe. Which is why, when I started writing this book, I was scratching my head wondering how to describe it.

But then I met Sanjeev Bikhchandani and Deep Kalra. And suddenly everything fell into place. Because in the half an hour that I spent with each of them, they gave me everything I needed. Of course, I added my own masala to it (I call it learning) and converted it into the inevitable acronym—PERFECT ATTITUDE. Which stands for:

P: PERSEVERING
E: ETHICAL
R: RESPONSIBLE
F: FLEXIBLE
E: Willing to do EVERYTHING
C: CUSTOMER-ORIENTED
T: BUILD TRUST

Sounds good, doesn't it? So, let's take up each of these one by one. Being CUSTOMER-ORIENTED—the 'C' in PERFECT—

doesn't need any explanation, does it. Your customer is the reason why you exist. If she doesn't come to you, you don't have a business. Period. So be aware of what she wants. Take feedback from her. Keep your ear to the ground. And have the FLEXIBILITY to pivot your business model. Look at iDream. When Covid hit the world, the customer (the student) could not go to school. So what did the founders of iDream do? Well, they made their content available online over the phone. Therefore, students who had access to a smartphone at home were able to access it. Or take a look at Instamojo. Over time, the founders realized that their customers did not just want payment solutions. They also wanted to get into e-commerce and sell their products and services online. And that's exactly what Instamojo allowed them to do, through the buyout of GetMeAShop. Please remember—be close to the customer, be flexible, and you are unlikely to go wrong.

And then, of course, we have 'P' for PERSEVERING. I think Sanjeev Bikhchandani put it brilliantly when he called it, '*Lambi* race *ka ghoda* (be in the game for the long run)'. Creating your start-up is not a two-year project, after which you take a sabbatical. It's a lifelong commitment. Sure, you'll have problems along the way. As Deep Kalra says, keep at it, keep pivoting if necessary. Your first business model might not work. The second one might not work either. But hopefully, somewhere along the line, things will fall into place. You may encounter problems along the way, which both Instamojo and iDream did, but those are part of the game. Just keep at it, and things could work out.

Now let me take the next three together, namely RESPONSIBLE, ETHICAL and BUILD TRUST (the 'R', 'E' and 'T' in the PERFECT ATTITUDE). I don't think I need to explain the word 'ethical'. But I need to spend a bit of time on the word 'responsible'. A DREAM Founder needs to take responsibility for his or her decisions and actions. If you've taken a decision and it goes wrong, what do you do? Blame someone else?

No way. Take responsibility for your decision or action. On the other hand, if something goes right, do you take all the credit? Of course not, my friend. Share it. In fact, give your team the lion's share of the credit. Only then will they trust you. And only then will they function like the highly motivated, charged-up team that they need to be.

Incidentally, this doesn't apply to employees alone. It applies to anyone who deals with you—whether it is partners, distributors, vendors, or just about anyone else. Give them a fair deal, be ethical in your dealings, take responsibility for your actions, and you'll build trust.

And now for the last bit in the PERFECT ATTITUDE—the second 'E', namely, the willingness to do EVERYTHING. Let me tell you a story to explain what I mean. M.M. Tandon (name changed), was a branch manager in one of the biggest, most respected FMCG companies in the country. As you might expect, the company used to attract wonderful talent, specifically MBAs from the IIMs. One such person—we'll call him Prakash—had just joined the company as a management trainee and was to work under the branch manager, Tandon.

Soon after Prakash joined, Tandon asked him to collect a bunch of posters from the company's store. These posters talked about the company's products. He also asked Prakash to pick up a bucket of glue, go around town and put up these posters at vantage points, where they would be visible to consumers.

As you can imagine, Prakash was aghast. 'Sir, I'm an MBA from one of the IIMs. How can you ask me to do this? Even an office boy could do it.'

Tandon tried to coax him into accepting this highly intellectual assignment, but Prakash was clear. He was willing to work hard, very hard, but this was way below his dignity. Of course, he said all this politely; after all, he had just joined. And so, the chapter was closed. Tandon gave Prakash another assignment, where he was to visit various kirana shops in the city, and try and book orders for the company's products. This was acceptable to our bright young MBA, and he trotted off to do what his boss had asked him to.

When Prakash reached the first kirana shop and was speaking to the owner, he noticed something. Some distance away, he could see a man carrying a bucket of glue and putting up posters on the walls. However, Prakash did not take notice and moved on to the next kirana shop. Once again, he saw the same man putting up posters. At the next shop, and the next. It was almost as though this man was following Prakash around. And when he reached the next shop and saw exactly the same thing happening, he couldn't stand the suspense any longer. He went up to the man who was putting up the posters.

And who did he see? M.M. Tandon!

Now what do you think our bright young MBA did? That's right—he apologized profusely to Tandon, took the bucket and posters from him and started putting them up himself. By the way, some years later, Tandon ultimately rose to become the chairman of the company—and perhaps one of the most successful chairmen the company ever had!

Now tell me, why was Tandon so keen to get Prakash to put up the posters? After all, the young man was right, even an office boy could have put them up. You certainly didn't need an MBA for that.

That, my friend, is a great question. Yes, an office boy could have easily done the job. But would he put up the posters too close to each other? In which case, he would have covered only a small geographical area. For all practical purposes, the posters would have been wasted. Or would he put them up too far apart? In which case, the customer would not get repeated views, and therefore, might not remember the products being advertised. Would he put them up close to competing products? What was the ideal height of the poster for visibility? Were there some places where they were guaranteed to be pulled down? As you can see, even for such a mundane task, there were important decisions to be taken and guidelines to be followed. And this is the key—in future, when Prakash sent his office boy to put up posters, he, Prakash, would need to brief him about these guidelines. But how could he, if he hadn't first done it himself?

You see, if you want your people to do something, you first need to do it yourself. That's the only way you will know what's happening, and that's the only way people will respect you and listen to you. I remember the MD of a company manufacturing tractors, who could take a tractor apart down to the last nut and bolt, and put it together again. And for this, he was hugely respected by his people. And, of course, he could guide them.

There are a few other reasons as well. Sometimes a task is unpalatable. No one wants to do it. In such cases you have no option—you've got to show the way. Please remember, no work is dirty work. Set an example that you would want others to follow.

By the way, don't get me wrong. I never said you should do everything all the time. You can't—you'll either die or go mad. As Deep Kalra has mentioned in the foreword, you must empower your people. Develop them, so that they grow and take on more and more responsibility. And that cannot happen if you try and do everything.

The point is that you *must be prepared* to do everything. Lead by example. Get your hands dirty. You cannot possibly build a successful empire by sitting in an air-conditioned ivory tower.

And that's what I had to share about the PERFECT ATTITUDE of a DREAM Founder. I've shared some examples of this in the current chapter. But there will be many more examples as you go through the book.

So read on . . .

Section II

The RIGHT TEAM

5

Please Get Yourself a Co-founder

Dear founder, we've discussed the fact that you need to DREAM BIG. But to EXECUTE this dream, you need to build the RIGHT TEAM, don't you? And that starts with your co-founder. Now, there is an obvious risk in building a start-up with a single founder. God forbid, if something were to happen to you, where does that leave your company? And if you've taken investors on board, where does that leave them? You see? There's an obvious benefit of having a co-founder, isn't there?

But there are many more benefits to having co-founders. And to understand these, let me tell you the story of MeraMundu.com.

Why You Need a Co-founder: The Story of MeraMundu

If you are familiar with Hindi, you would know that *mundu* means helper. Of course, if you're not, you've just learnt a new Hindi word (and thanks for the thanks)! A mundu is a young, low-skilled worker. Often used as a delivery boy. For instance, you might say to him, 'Mundu, market *se* bread *le aa*', and the mundu would obediently go to the market and get bread for you. Or you might tell him, 'Mundu, *yeh* packet *Ganjoo sahib ke ghar de de*', and your mundu would deliver the packet to Mr Ganjoo. Small, local deliveries, you see?

Of course, you are aware of Dunzo, one of the market leaders in this space. But then, Dunzo cannot be everywhere. It can be in Mumbai and Delhi, but it cannot be in Jhumri Telaiya. Or Uluberia. Or Sibsagar. Or Saproon. Or the tens of thousands—perhaps lakhs—of other small towns in India. And that's the opportunity MeraMundu wanted to tap. To be the delivery boy in these small towns.

MeraMundu was started by two friends, who we will simply refer to by their nicknames, Taara and Pyaara. You see, their real names—the ones on their respective Aadhaar cards—were long and complex, and even I couldn't figure them out. Now, Taara was great at anything to do with sales or marketing. When he was all of three years old, he had convinced his mother that chocolates were far healthier for him than milk. At the age of fifteen, his father had had a chat with him about the need to get good marks in his board exams. And had gone away convinced that becoming a professional cricketer was a far better option for his son. I have known Taara for many years and there are many more stories that I could tell you, but you get the idea, don't you? Taara was a crack sales guy. Over time, he had also mastered the subject of digital marketing. Therefore, when MeraMundu was launched, it was quite natural that he took on the responsibility of marketing (remember our BOMB approach to execution?).

On the other hand, Pyaara was poor at sales. But he was a whiz at organizing things. While in school, he organized sporting events. In college, he was usually in the thick of organizing any college festival—and he did so extremely successfully. He also organized all the mass bunks (and believe me, that's not easy with two or three guys sneaking into class behind your back. Those guys who actually believe that college is meant to study in). Yes sir, Pyaara was great at organizing stuff. And so, it was quite natural that he took charge of operations (remember BOMB again?).

Now, please pause for a moment and think about what I've just said. Co-founders need to bring different capabilities to the table. In this case, Taara brought in sales and marketing, whereas Pyaara brought in operations. They happily split responsibilities in the same manner. And that, my friend, is one of the major benefits of having a co-founder!

But that's not all. Before finalizing on any marketing campaign, Taara would first run it past Pyaara. So, what if Pyaara was not a marketing guy? He could at least examine the campaign critically, couldn't he? And the best part was that he would ask tough questions. On the other hand, when Pyaara figured out how to manage logistics for his delivery boys, Taara was called in to give his comments. They didn't always agree. But that was great, because each of them got another viewpoint before taking any major decision.

And then, of course, the big day arrived when the two needed to raise funds. Taara was the obvious choice since it involved selling the concept to investors. But it wasn't an easy job. No sir, it was highly time-consuming. The angel investors wanted more and more meetings, and more and more details. They wanted to spend lots of time on the business model. They wanted to meet customers. They grilled Taara repeatedly. And it wasn't just one group of angels. Taara had spoken to four angel networks and all these discussions were proceeding concurrently. You can imagine the result—Taara was going bonkers. Almost all his time went into investor meetings. Very little into running the company.

So, who managed the company during this time?

Pyaara, of course! Yes, major marketing decisions were still made by Taara. But the nitty-gritties were handled by Pyaara. And that's another message for you, dear reader. Fundraising is a tough, time-consuming process. If there is only one founder, what does he do? Does he focus on fundraising? In which case, the company remains headless. Or does he spend time running the company? In which case, fundraising may not happen. You see the benefits of a co-founder?

Now I'm sure you have a question, and you're right, it's a great question. What if you were to have a senior-level employee instead of a co-founder? Perhaps with some ESOPs (employee stock ownership plans)? Wouldn't that work as well as a co-founder?

Of course not! Don't be silly. Founders and co-founders are permanent. They stick around through thick and thin. Because it is their company, their baby. Because each of them has a significant stake in the company. Whereas an employee can leave at any time. 'Bad times? No problem. I'll just look for another job, thank you very much. Anyway, my ESOPs are tiny—let them go.' And so, you get the message, don't you? An employee, no matter how good he or she is, cannot replace a co-founder.

But here's the twist. Over time, an employee can become a co-founder. Once you've got a chance to work closely with him, you begin to understand his strengths and weaknesses. And hopefully trust him. You could then decide if he's the right co-founder for you. If you do take him on, give him significant ESOPs. And that's it—you've got yourself a co-founder!

But who is that ideal character? What should he (or she) be like? What traits should he (or she) possess?

Well, to get the answer, just read on . . .

Who Is the Right Co-founder?

Right from the title of this book, I've been talking about DREAM Founders. Now if you have a co-founder (or more) in the company, I'm sure you would agree that the title applies to both. Obvious, isn't it? You cannot have one DREAM Founder and the other one with just the wrong attitude. Or someone who simply cannot get into execution mode. Or a person who doesn't take responsibility for his actions. Right? So that much is clear— both need to be DREAM Founders.

The other critical issue is trust. For co-founders to work together successfully, they must trust each other. I would go so far as to say that trust is perhaps the most important thing between them. Just imagine what would happen, if one co-founder were constantly worried about the other one siphoning off money from the company.

And, of course, as you've seen in the story of MeraMundu, co-founders should bring complementary capabilities to the table. If one is great at strategizing, the other one should be able to tackle operations. If one is a marketing whiz, the other one should be a tech cat. And so on.

But there is something more. Something extremely important. So important, that I decided to devote a full section to it. The next one . . .

The Need for a Shared Dream

Let me tell you the story of Akela and Dukela. These two young men were having a heart-to-heart chat in a nearby café. And no, this was not just their usual argument, which took place virtually every day. Leaving them fretting and fuming, with one of them walking out of their tiny conference room in a huff. No, this one was more serious. Because this time . . .

But hang on. I have this habit of getting carried away. And I'm sure you have no clue what I'm talking about. So, let's take a deep breath and get back to the beginning of the story. You see, Akela and Dukela were childhood friends and had co-founded a start-up. Yes, they were close friends, but there was one small issue. Akela was extremely ambitious and his dream was to create a rapidly growing, highly scalable start-up. If that meant a high cash burn, so be it. Given the growth in his start-up, he was confident that he would be able to get the appropriate funding to compensate for the cash burn. Dukela, on the other hand, came from a more conservative family. Both his parents were mid-level government officials, and the buzzword at home—or rather the three buzzwords—were save, save, save. Rarely would the family splurge on an expensive holiday. Even their outings to restaurants were restricted to the local halwai. And as in many Indian families,

Dukela had imbibed these values of thrift. Anyhow, the two were fast friends and they were sure they would be able to sort out any differences. In any case, two human beings would always have differences, wouldn't they?

After the usual high-intensity debates and discussions, they decided to create a start-up providing home maintenance services, along the lines of Urban Company. Fortunately, they had read my earlier book *Funding Your Start-Up: And Other Nightmares*, and they realized that they could not possibly compete with a giant like Urban Company. Which meant that metros such as Mumbai, Delhi and Bangalore were out. That's right, they were clear that they would operate in smaller towns. And what better place to start than their hometown, Kanpur, in Uttar Pradesh?

Our friends were able to put together 5 lakh from their savings. Of course, they also begged and borrowed from their chacha and *mama*. Fortunately, they had had the sense to maintain good relations with these relatives of theirs. Consequently, both the chacha and mama responded by putting in a couple of lakhs each. And so, after selecting an auspicious date on the advice of the family pandit, their start-up, Mistriji, was launched.

The two friends were hard-working and business was decent. But very soon, Akela began to dream big. 'Yaar, this is too tiny a business. We need to expand into other towns in UP—Agra, Benares, Gorakhpur, Aligarh—the world is just waiting for us.'

'But what about the money?' asked Dukela. 'We are burning a couple of lakhs of cash every month.'

'Oh, we'll raise funds. Shouldn't be a problem.'

Dukela was not convinced. Yes, his dream was to build a growing business, but one that was sustainable. Not one where they kept burning loads of cash every month. 'I think we should first make the business viable, and only then grow. Let's just focus on Kanpur for the moment. If that means we grow more slowly, that's OK,' was Dukela's view.

However, Akela was in no mood to listen. And in any case, he was far more aggressive than Dukela. Of course, you can figure out what happened. The two of them raised 50 lakh and quickly expanded to both Agra and Aligarh. The result? The burn increased to 5 lakh per month.

As you can imagine, with this kind of burn, the young friends soon ran out of cash. And therefore, a second fundraiser became inevitable. But by now Akela had tasted blood. 'Yaar, we now need to expand into all towns of UP—Bulandshahar, Saharanpur, Mathura, we'll just sweep the state. I've done a quick calculation—we'll raise three crores this time.'

Dukela was aghast. 'Do you realize what that will do to our cash burn?'

'I know, it'll go up. But that's the only way to go. We must become market leaders, and for that, we simply have to scale rapidly.'

As usual, Dukela protested, but once again his objections were brushed aside. And Akela went back to investors to raise the money. However, by now, there was a visible strain between the two friends. Dukela was extremely unhappy, but he realized there was little he could do about it. And by the way, just in case you thought fundraising was the only issue on which the friends disagreed, please think again. They even began to fight over trivial issues, such as the location of the new coffee vending machine in the office.

But one day, it became just too much. And that's when the two of them decided to have a heart-to-heart chat in the nearby café. For a change, it was not in the bar next door—after all, they had to be sober to discuss such vital issues. And that's where this story began (if you've forgotten, please go back and read the story again—don't ask me to keep repeating myself).

Dukela was the first to speak. 'Look bhai, we have been close friends all our life. But things are not okay right now.'

'Yes, I can see that,' said Akela, quietly. 'But don't worry. Once we become market leaders, everything will sort itself out.'

'No, bhai. I'm not happy with the way things are going. Too much cash burn, repeated need for funding. That's not the kind of company I thought we would create.'

There was silence for a bit. And then Dukela took a deep breath, as though coming to a decision. 'Akela, I would like to quit.'

'Quit?' asked Akela, absolutely shocked. 'How can you quit? We have been close friends all along. We started this company together with a dream. How can you leave me in the lurch now? You can't do this to me!' And Akela was almost shouting!

'Bhai, that is where we made a mistake. Because we did not have a shared dream. You have always been super ambitious, and wanted to build a rapidly growing company. If that meant a huge cash burn, too bad. You would get funding. My dream, on the other hand, was to build a self-sustaining company. Where we wouldn't have to lie awake at night, wondering whether or not we would get funding. And whether we would need to close down the company if we didn't get the funding we needed. No, bhai, we definitely did not have a shared dream. And that's where we went wrong.'

Akela was quiet. There were lots of things he wanted to say, but somehow he wasn't able to. Dukela had just said it all, and deep down, Akela agreed with him.

So, the two friends parted ways. And that's the message I want to leave you with, dear reader. Please remember this. Yes, you should get a co-founder for your start-up. But please, please, please ensure that both of you (or all of you, if there are more) share the same dream. Things are tough enough as it is. Don't make them tougher.

One Request

Finally, before I end this story, I have a request. Dukela is currently looking for a job. He's a very hardworking person—I can vouch for that. So, if you are aware of an opportunity where he can fit in, do let me know. I'll put him in touch with you.

6

Too Many Cooks—Sorry, Co-founders

Now that you've read the previous chapter, you would be aware that it is good to have a co-founder. Or even two.

But hang on. If co-founders are so good to have around, why not five of them? Or more?

Aha, my friend. That won't do. And to understand why, let me share with you the story of Garamkhaana. Haven't heard the name? Well, that's not surprising—after all, I just made it up a few minutes ago. The story is completely true, it's just that the name of the start-up has been changed. Anyhow, to continue with the story, Garamkhaana was a food delivery start-up in Bangalore. And I'm talking about the heyday of food delivery, when you had lots of start-ups in this space. Not just Zomato and Swiggy, but also Foodpanda, TinyOwl, Tinmen, and a host of other kids on the block. Yes, my friend, for millennials who did not want to cook, and who did not have the time to go to restaurants every night, food delivery was just what the doctor ordered. Hundreds of food delivery start-ups were launched, each claiming to have a different business model and a completely unique offering. But, of course, you know all this, so I don't need to repeat it. What you do need to know, is that Garamkhaana was one of these start-ups.

Now, here's the interesting part. Garamkhaana had five co-founders. Yes, you heard that right, it had five co-founders.

All five were batchmates and close friends from the same engineering college. They would play cricket together, they would watch movies together, they even studied together— occasionally, that is, when they decided to study. So, when a start-up was to be launched, it was only natural that they would launch it together. One last thing—I haven't introduced them yet, so please meet Arun, Varun, Tarun, Karun and Barun.

It was so exciting. Five close friends, starting a company and growing it together. Of course, they had to allocate responsibilities between them, which they managed to do. Arun was the clear leader among them, so it was natural for him to don the mantle of CEO. He also looked after sales and marketing. Varun was good at operations. In fact, he had been one of the organizers of their intercollege festival. Quite naturally, the responsibility for operations fell into his lap. Tarun's role was clear—he was the whiz programmer among the lot, and therefore he was responsible for tech.

So far so good. But what about the other two? What about Karun and Barun? Now, Karun was also good at relationships, which probably meant that he would also be good at sales, and therefore at onboarding restaurants and cloud kitchens. But that was already the responsibility of the CEO, Arun. Anyhow, the team decided in one of their 'strategic beer meetings', that onboarding restaurants was critical to their success and therefore, both Karun and Arun would be responsible for this. Between them, they could decide which parts of the city each would handle.

And then we had Barun. Again, a very good programmer, but you couldn't have two people leading the tech team, could you? Anyhow, Barun did not have any other skills, and he had to be accommodated—after all, he was a director of the company. So, he and Tarun were made jointly responsible for the tech platform.

Dear reader, I would now like you to pause for a moment and think. Can you see what was happening? No? Well then, please splash water on your face and get a strong mug of black coffee. Isn't it obvious? Five founders, each of them a director, but they didn't have clear roles for each of them. Three founders would probably have been ideal—one each for sales and marketing, operations and tech. But they had no choice. After all, there were five of them!

Anyhow, the business started off. Our friends were also able to raise a bit of funding from angel investors. But they soon realized that they were in a highly competitive space, with lots of other young founders trying to jump on to the food delivery bandwagon. To compete, the friends would have to operate with very low margins. Their cash burn was fairly high, and the funds they had raised from angels were depleting rapidly. Tough times called for tough measures, and, unfortunately, they had to let go of some of their people. But still the cash burn continued. And so, in their next strategic beer meeting, Arun decided to take a tough stand. 'Guys, we cannot carry on like this. The cash burn simply must be reduced. As directors, I think each of us will need to take a 50 per cent cut in salary.'

There was silence all around, intermingled with horror. Tarun was the first to speak. 'Arun, I cannot manage with less. You guys are aware that I'm staying as a PG (paying guest). As it is, I'm finding it tough. No way.'

Karun nodded in agreement, 'Same here.'

Varun looked a little uncomfortable. 'I've just bought a Royal Enfield bike and I'm paying the instalments. Sorry, can't manage either.' Saying which, he looked a bit sheepish.

Barun looked around at the others. 'Guys, if the three of you cannot take a dip in salary, isn't it unfair to ask me to do so?' And, by the way, had you been there, you would have noticed a bit of belligerence in the usually mild Barun.

That, of course, left Arun. 'Look, I can take a bit of a cut, but I agree with Barun. We are all equal shareholders, and if a cut has to be taken, it cannot be only the two of us.' There was, of course, a heated debate and discussion, but you can imagine what the end result was. Lots of beer, but no salary cuts. And please remember, salaries are fixed costs. Costs that are incurred, whether you get revenues or not. You see? Variable costs such as incentives or commissions are paid out only when you get corresponding revenues. But fixed costs are fixed costs. That's why they are called fixed costs!

Dear reader, I hope you get the message. Not only did these founders have overlapping responsibilities, but they also had a hefty fixed salary bill, which could not be reduced. Five people with overlapping responsibilities, who had to be paid their full salary every month. You see the problem?

But there is more, so fill up your cup of coffee and read on. This situation, where two of the founders were willing to take a cut in salary but three others were unwilling, was clearly untenable. Soon the founders started fighting among themselves. Some were in favour of selling out to one of the big boys such as Swiggy or Zomato. But the others would have none of it. After all, it was their baby, so how could they possibly sell out? Two of them were in favour of pivoting the business model towards delivering other stuff, something along the lines of Dunzo. But again, the others were dead against this. 'Come on, guys. We started a business in the food delivery space. How can we get into delivering babies' diapers?' So that didn't work either.

The disagreements became more and more bitter. And then one day, it had to happen. Tarun and Karun decided to quit and take up jobs. It was becoming tough to pay their PG rent, and anyway, they had had enough of entrepreneurship—thank you very much!

Arun, Varun and Barun tried desperately to raise some funding to survive, but by then, it was too late. Sadly, the three friends that were left had to shut down the business. Sadder but much, much wiser. Too many founders—not a great idea.

But the story does not end there. Soon after, Arun had another strategic beer meeting. But not with his co-founders. This time, he had a meeting with his mentor—yes, the same bearded professor I spoke about in the introduction.

As you can imagine, Arun poured his heart out to his mentor. 'Sir, we made a mistake. Too many founders. Too much of a fixed salary bill without enough work for all of us. Not a viable option. We should not have had more than three—one for marketing, one for operations, and one for tech. And in any case, with so many founders we always had disagreements, sometimes violent ones. We made a mistake.' Saying which, he took a long, sad swig of his beer.

But the professor had other ideas. Always positive, this is what he had to say, 'Yes, young man, you might have made a mistake. But you've learnt a lot, haven't you? And therefore, you won't make the same mistake next time. Also, remember, investors love to invest in founders with experience. Even those who have blundered but have learnt from their mistakes. *Kahaani abhi baaki hai, mere dost* (there is lots more to your story, my friend).'

Arun looked up from his mug. Yes, that was true. He had learnt a lot. And he was determined to use this learning in his next start-up. Gradually, as more and more mugs of beer went down his alimentary canal, the dejection changed into hope. Finally, a somewhat sloshed but visibly brighter Arun raised his mug and said, 'Thank you, shir. Sh-sh-sheers!'

7

Add the Right People

So, we've looked at co-founders as the first step in building the RIGHT TEAM. And now, let's move on to the rest of the gang—the managers, the programmers, the operations team, the marketing guys, etc. That's right, we will now look at the subject of recruitment. And the key question here is: How do you figure out who the right person is?

Well, you've already seen what iDream and Instamojo did. They were both extremely selective about any candidate they took on. The person had to believe in what the company was doing. She wasn't applying for a typical job. No, she had to share in the dream. The vibes had to be positive. And so on . . .

But there are a few more things that you can learn from the real masters. Things that even experienced recruiters are not aware of. And in this context, one person who has always impressed me is my young friend, Mehringez F. Deliverywala. Now, I realize that this name is very long and cumbersome, so from here on, I'll drop the 'F' and just use the much shorter and more convenient Mehringez Deliverywala. In fact, when I get tired, I'll just call her Mehri, and I hope you'll understand. So here are some stories about how this young lady recruited people.

Mehringez was the proud founder of Wedeliver, one of the leading start-ups in India in the logistics space. For those of you who are not aware of the company—and frankly, I'm surprised you aren't—this Delhi-based company was in the business of delivering anything. From chocolates to groceries, to soft toys, to medicines, to Diwali gifts, to just about anything else. Typically, Wedeliver would tie up with e-commerce companies and deliver their packages to their customers. Now I could go on and on about what it did, but that's not important for the purposes of this book. What is important is how this young lady recruited her team. So let me take you through some of her interviews. And let's see how much you can learn from her . . .

The First Interview: Identifying the Deserter

Our first story begins with our friend Mehringez recruiting someone to head sales. An extremely critical position, because the company's future business depended on this one person. No sales, no revenues, and no company, you see? So, let's peep into the one conference room that the company boasted of, where she was conducting an interview. Across the table, of course, sat the candidate, B.K. Bahaana.

Now, Bahaana was a crack sales guy. He had just the right experience. And a history of meeting targets, which is not too common among this breed. By the way, this also gave him a bit of a swagger, but then who would grudge him that? He sat across the table with just a wee bit of attitude, looking as though he had already got the job, and it was up to him to take it or leave it. And, by the way, he *had* got the job—well, almost. Because Mehringez was extremely impressed with what she saw and had more or less made up her mind.

However, over the years she had learnt to ask candidates questions about their weaknesses and failures, so that's what she did. Of course, the candidate was almost selected, but just for the record, it wouldn't hurt to ask him about his failures.

'Can you give me an example of a deal that you lost, and why? And what you learnt from it?'

'Sure,' said Bahaana, as he took a sip of his coffee. 'I had almost closed an order with a manufacturing company. But they wanted a discount of 5 per cent, which my CEO refused to give. My competitor's quote was lower than mine.' And with that, Bahaana washed his hands off all responsibility. Clearly, it was not his failure—the problem was the price.

This sounded logical, but somehow, somewhere, at the back of her head, Mehringez heard faint warning bells. She decided to pursue the topic further.

'So, if your quote had been at par with that of your competitor, you would have won the contract?'

'Of course. I've rarely lost orders,' was the response.

By now the bell was pealing a bit louder and Mehringez realized she was on to something, so she pressed on.

'Did you ever have any problems with anyone who reported to you?'

'Yes. A few months ago, I had a sales guy called Mehnat Kumar reporting to me. But he was very, *very* unlike his name (for those who do not understand Hindi, *mehnat* means hard work). Completely lethargic. No initiative. Can't have a sales guy like that.'

'So, did you try and get him to change?'

'Of course. In fact, I've been able to turn around several such people. But this guy was beyond changing. Entirely his fault.'

By now, Mehringez had realized the problem. A few more similar questions, and she put her palms on the table and said, 'Okay, thanks a lot, Bahaana. We'll get back to you.'

Somewhat surprised, Bahaana nodded. His credentials were impeccable. The interview had gone off well. And he was a bit surprised that he hadn't got an offer on the spot. 'Maybe these guys are bureaucratic and will take time,' he thought to himself. 'Pity.

As a start-up, they need to be quick decision makers. Anyway, not my problem.' And with that, he walked out of the office.

But he was wrong. Totally wrong. Mehringez was a very quick decision maker. She had decided not to take on Bahaana despite his impressive credentials. And I'm sure you've guessed why. Anyhow, that evening, she happened to go to a party where she met an old friend. Now, in case you didn't know it, this friend also ran an interesting start-up. So, chilled wine in hand, the two of them started comparing notes.

'How's your recruitment going on?' asked Mehringez.

'Oh, great,' was the immediate response. 'In fact, a couple of months ago, we took on a young man with a very interesting name—Mehnat Kumar. Never heard the name before.'

Suddenly, Mehringez was interested. Trying to sound casual, she asked, 'How is he doing?'

'He's brilliant. Extremely motivated, very hard-working, exactly what his name suggests.'

After a while, they veered around to other topics. But as you can imagine, Mehringez's mind was elsewhere. She was thinking about what her mentor, the bearded professor, had once told her, 'Never take on a person who doesn't take responsibility for his actions. If you find someone who is constantly shifting the blame away from himself, that's a dangerous person to have in your team. Remember, it's not just the DREAM Founder who needs to have the right attitude. It's the employees as well. And one key aspect of attitude, is the willingness to take responsibility. If you've made a mistake, if you've failed, own up. Don't blame someone else. Incidentally, there is a term that we use for people who don't take responsibility. We call them "deserters".'

The more she thought about it, the more Mehringez realized the value of the professor's words. And quietly, without anyone noticing it, she raised her wine glass, smiled, and said ever so softly, 'Thank you, Prof.'

The Second Interview: Attention to Detail

The interview was in progress, and the candidate was extremely promising. Jugaad Gupta, for that was his name, was being interviewed for a senior position in the operations department of Wedeliver. Mehringez was one of the interviewers, along with Manjit Senior Singh, the head of operations in the company. A power-packed interview panel, as you can see. Manjit had already met Jugaad and had been extremely impressed with him. Just the right kind of experience with their closest competitor, Chaotic. Along with his team, he had been instrumental in growing Chaotic's business fivefold in the past year. All questions Manjit asked had been answered with supreme confidence. Here was a guy who understood operations, and would do a great job. And Manjit was desperately short of someone to help him manage operations. Business was growing rapidly, and he could not manage on his own. As you can imagine, therefore, he was very keen to induct Jugaad into the organization.

Even Mehringez was impressed. Jugaad did have a strong background, and his experience was relevant. Plus, he seemed to be a good manager. The interview was going well, and Manjit began to dream of the time when he would be able to put up his feet and relax with a beer. At least once in six months. After all, he would now have support.

There was, however, one niggling issue that kept bothering Mehringez. 'Jugaad, you say you have worked with Chaotic for nearly four years. But according to your résumé, you joined in April 2018. And it's now 2020. That's only two years.'

'No ma'am, that's not correct. I joined in April 2016.'

'Take a look at your résumé,' said Mehringez, as she handed it over.

'Oh, that's a typographic error,' was the immediate response from Jugaad, as he looked at the offending document. And with that, the issue was brushed aside.

'Jugaad, your résumé is a critical document. How could you make a mistake here?' asked Mehringez, as she looked meaningfully at Manjit.

'Actually, I was extremely busy, so I had to write this résumé late at night. I must have been tired. But my experience is all valid!'

'I see,' said Mehringez, although the way she said it, she clearly didn't see.

'By the way, the name of your current employer is Chaotic Pvt Ltd, isn't it? But your résumé says Choratic. Take a look.' And she handed over the résumé to Jugaad once more.

'Ah yes, a minor typing error once again. But these are matters of detail. Please look at my work, my experience. You'll find those extremely relevant.'

'Yes, of course,' said Mehringez, nodding her head absently as if she agreed. But a close observer would have noticed that she did not agree. There were other issues in the résumé as well, such as basic formatting errors. The indentation would vary for no reason at all. So would the font size. No sir, the résumé was badly drafted. Perhaps Jugaad didn't have time. But for a document as critical as his résumé, *shouldn't he have made time*?

'Jugaad, would you let us discuss your case for a few minutes? Please wait outside this room.' Saying which, Mehringez opened the door and politely let Jugaad out.

Now that the two were alone, Manjit pounced on his boss. 'Come on, Mehri, these are minor issues. He must have been in a hurry when he wrote his CV. Just look at his experience. Completely relevant. And please remember, we are in a desperate situation right now. We've got to take him on . . .'

You can imagine what followed. There was a reasonably heated argument between the two, with Manjit almost threatening to walk out of the room. Finally, Mehringez relented and Manjit had his way. Jugaad was called in and the offer was made. And in one month he joined and was a proud member of the Wedeliver team.

Now, you thought that was the end of the story, didn't you? Ha, ha, my friend, think again. A few weeks later, Mehringez and Manjit had gone out to a nearby café for—what else—coffee, of course. And Manjit had a worried look on his face.

'What's up, Manjit?'

'I don't know, Mehri. Something's not quite right.'

'What? Tell me.'

'Well, there seem to be a lot of mistakes in our deliveries. Packages for Connaught Place land up in Vasant Vihar. Packages for Greater Kailash land up in Karol Bagh. Sometimes, packages are sent half-open and the customer is wild. Can't understand it. We used to have blunders earlier, but certainly not so many.'

Suddenly, Mehringez's favourite coffee didn't taste so great. 'That's bad,' she said, looking equally worried. And then she had a thought, 'Who is handling all this? Isn't it Jugaad?'

'That's right.'

And then it hit Manjit. 'Of course. The carelessly drafted résumé. Now I remember why you were not keen to take him on,' he said, a bit sheepishly. After all, it was only because of his tantrums that Mehringez had finally relented.

And as he squirmed in his seat, looking most uncomfortable, Mehringez had the last word. 'Manjit, you must remember, attention to detail is critical in any job—whether it is sales, operations, marketing, or just about anything else. Otherwise, you cannot bank on the person. You need to keep checking what he's doing, just to clean up the mess. And that's a huge overhead. After all, you need people who you can rely on, don't you?'

Manjit nodded, desperately wanting to get away, as Mehringez went on, 'Unfortunately, lack of attention to detail is an attitude. Sometimes we call it a *chalta hai* (anything goes) attitude. And if a person doesn't have attention to detail, it's not easy to get him to build it up. It is possible, but it's a long process, with you as the boss having to put in major effort. So why take on such a person at all?

'Incidentally, I have found that the résumé is a great place to check this. If there are errors—even small ones, such as formatting errors—that's a clear sign of danger. After all, a résumé is such an important document. And if there is no attention to detail in the résumé, well, what else can you say about the candidate?'

As usual, of course, Manjit had the last word. 'Yes boss,' was all he could say.

The Third Interview: Take on Hungry People

It was recruitment time at Wedeliver once again. This time, the company needed to recruit programmers. And that is why their seniormost tech person, Java Gupta, sat at his desk along with their best programmer, Python Jha—to interview potential programmers.

Now, Wedeliver was a small company, but it was growing rapidly and therefore they attracted decent talent. The problem, of course, was that decent talent was rarely stable. The good guys would find another job within a year or at best two, and that was the end of the association. Of course, given that software developers were notorious for not documenting anything, this also meant that the guy who took over lost a decent amount of hair in trying to figure out what the earlier person had been doing. Also, the good guys would demand more than good salaries. And ESOPs as well. But, of course, Wedeliver accepted that as part of the game.

Anyhow, to get back to the interviews. Wedeliver had several good candidates applying for the jobs available. There were young men and women from several good National Institutes of Technology, or NITs (earlier called regional engineering colleges). And some MCAs (Master of Computer Applications) as well. There were even a couple of youngsters from one of the IITs. Naturally therefore, Java Gupta was quite excited. Today promised to be a good day.

And so the interviews began. Some candidates were shortlisted for Mehringez to take a final look, and others were eliminated. But that's not really of interest to us. What *is* of interest, however, is that one young man sitting patiently in the corner of the reception waiting for his turn (I hope you've noticed him). And when all the other interviews were over, Java realized that this person was still left. No one knew how he had been called for the interview—his résumé said that he was not even a graduate, and was currently doing his BA by correspondence. It was probably a mistake. Such a waste of time for everyone. However, since he had been called, there was no option but to interview him. And so Bhola Nath, for that was his name, was called in, perhaps for two minutes, just to complete the formalities and reject him.

Strangely, however, the interview did not end in two minutes. It actually went on for twenty minutes. The interviewers were impressed with the steely determination of the young man. His communication was poor, of course. And he was effectively just a school pass-out. Not even a graduate. How could they possibly recruit him? How would he jell with the others in the organization? Would they make fun of him? There were just too many issues. However, he was a very good programmer, so after a lot of debate, the interviewers decided to leave the decision to Mehringez.

Now Mehringez was in a tearing hurry that day. There was a problem with one major client, and she was preoccupied. She simply rushed through the final round of interviews. Till at last she came to Bhola. 'Why are you wasting my time with this guy? He is still doing his graduation. And that too, by correspondence. Please send him off,' she said impatiently.

'Mehri, just spend two minutes with this guy. And you'll realize why we put him up to you,' was the response.

'OK, but I'm telling you, it's a waste of time.' Saying which, Mehringez called Bhola to her desk. Impatient to get it over with, she asked him why he was doing his BA by correspondence, and not through regular college. And gradually the story came out. Bhola's father had a small paan–beedi shop tucked away in a corner of Chandni Chowk in Delhi. Unfortunately, his father had been unwell for years and could not attend to the shop. And therefore, Bhola and his brother had taken it over to keep the family income going. Obviously, that meant that Bhola could not attend regular college. But he was determined to get a degree, which was why he had enrolled himself in a correspondence course.

Despite her preoccupation with the client, Mehringez was impressed. 'So why do you want to take up this job instead of managing your shop?'

And the answer really hit her. 'Ma'am, I am keen to do something in life. My family has always been managing this shop, but I want to go beyond that. And believe me, I know I can. I just need one opportunity to prove myself.'

Now you can probably guess Mehringez's reaction. That's right, she believed this sincere young man. And over the next ten minutes—yes, Mehringez was willing to give him ten minutes out of her busy schedule— her conviction only strengthened. Till at the end, she said, 'Look, we can give you a chance. But we can't pay you much. It would upset our salary structure, since you are not even a graduate.'

'No problem, ma'am,' was the excited response. 'All I want is a chance to prove myself.' And you could see the gleam in Bhola's eyes as he shook hands with Mehringez and walked out of the room.

I'm sure you can guess what happened in the months and years that followed. Our young man Bhola was utterly inexhaustible. When the other programmers would take a break and go out for a smoke, or even a cold drink, he would be glued to his laptop. Where the others took vacations and went off to Shimla or Mussoorie, he would simply sit in front of his laptop and program. When everyone had left the office late at night and the chowkidar came to lock up, Bhola would plead with him to give him just a few more minutes. So much so that the chowkidar once remarked, '*Bhola bhai, aap sotey kab ho* (When do you sleep)?'

As the months went by, Mehringez realized that she had picked up a true gem. The other programmers would resign and leave, and new ones would take their place, but not Bhola. No way. At the time of writing this book, young Bhola had been with Wedeliver for three years and was clearly their most respected software developer. He would advise and guide the other programmers. And they all looked up to him.

And by the way, our young founder Mehringez had learnt something in life from this experience. 'Take on hungry people,' she would say. People who are desperate for an opportunity to prove themselves. They could be underqualified people, or those from a humble family background, or anyone else for whom life has not been a bed of roses. It's not always easy to locate such people. It takes a lot more effort. But if you do manage to locate them, they are the ones who will give it everything they've got. And they will form the backbone of your organization.'

Well said, Mehri!

8

But Don't Mess with Salaries

So far you've heard stories about Mehringez, and how she was great at getting together just the RIGHT TEAM. But there is one more story I must tell you. Actually, there are two stories—one about Mehringez, and another one about her twin sister Behringez, or Behri for short (that's right, they had very similar-sounding names. No law against it, is there?). Now, where Mehringez had created her start-up Wedeliver, Behringez had created a start-up called Justforkicks.

What did this start-up do? Guys, please don't ask me irrelevant questions. It doesn't really matter, does it? What does matter, and therefore what I want to share with you here, is how these two ladies tackled the burning issue of fixing salaries when recruiting people. And we'll start with Behringez.

The Story of Behringez

The candidate, Jaineel, was good. Really good. He was clearly a terrific programmer and he could answer all the questions that were thrown at him. And our young founder and CEO, Behringez, was becoming more and more convinced that he was just the right person to take into her organization. He was a simple graduate, which was actually good, because he would not have the airs of a typical MBA or even an engineer, and was more likely to be stable.

71

And so, half an hour later, Behringez had decided. 'We're taking on this guy,' she said to herself.

Of course, there was a small matter of salary. 'How much are you expecting?' asked Behringez.

'A lakh a month,' was the immediate answer.

Behringez almost jumped. 'A lakh a month? But you're a graduate with a couple of years of experience. That's the kind of money we pay our MBAs.'

However, Jaineel was adamant. 'That's what I expect,' he said, as if to say, take it or leave it.

'Okay, give me a few minutes—please wait outside.'

Once Jaineel was outside the conference room, Behringez started thinking. 'He's a good guy. Great addition to the team. Even though our existing guys with similar experience get just sixty thousand per month, he is worth it. And anyway, we can afford his salary . . .'

And so, the decision was made. Jaineel was called in and made an offer of Rs 1 lakh a month, which he accepted (who wouldn't?). One month later, he joined the start-up. Of course, as Behringez had expected, he was very good. And life carried on.

Till a few days later when Swati—one of her best programmers—came into Behringez's room. 'Behri, I want to leave.'

'But why?' asked Behringez. 'You've been with us for over two years, and you've been getting more and more responsibilities. You've been learning right through. I thought you were happy here. Why do you want to leave?'

Swati looked a little uncomfortable. 'Behri, *do saal ho gaye hain* (it's been two years). I need a change.'

As you might imagine, Behringez used all her powers of persuasion to convince the young Swati. But I'm sure you can figure out what happened. That's right, Swati was very pleasant, very polite, but adamant. She would leave, and that was final.

Since she had no choice, Behringez had to accept her decision. Anyhow, over time, things started getting back to normal. When, all of a sudden, Chetan, another great programmer, also put in his papers.

'My god, what's happening!' exclaimed Behringez angrily.

'Behri, I've got a better opportunity.'

'But why did you need to look around? You've been with us for three years. And you have been growing. What more could you ask for?'

'Yes Behri, but I think I need a change.'

That was all Behringez could get out of Chetan. Visibly angry by now, she glared at everyone around her. And that's when she noticed Manish, a third programmer, standing timidly next to her. 'Behri, can I speak to you in private?'

That was the last straw. The third resignation in a month. As you can imagine, Behringez was in a towering rage by now. The only thing that could help her cool down was a nice, hot cup of masala chai. The kind that Sunil, the office boy, made. But, of course, Sunil had other ideas. His answer was brief and to the point. 'Madam ji, *doodh khatam ho gaya hai* (there is no milk left),' was his chirpy reply.

Dear reader, we can discuss the impact of this innocent-sounding statement on Behri's blood pressure. But that's not our purpose here. Our purpose, very simply, is to understand why so many people were leaving Behringez. And she was determined to get the answer this time. She called Manish into the conference room and asked him point-blank, 'What is the issue, Manish? Is it salary?'

Manish was silent.

'Come on, Manish. If you've decided to leave, I won't stop you. But at least tell me, is it salary?'

'Behri, I was quite happy till a month ago. But Jaineel . . .'

And suddenly, it hit Behringez, 'You mean Jaineel's salary?'

'Yes, Behri. I have the same level of experience as him. I've been around for a year now. But you've given him a much higher salary than mine.'

Behringez slumped in her seat. 'And what about Chetan and Swati? Was it the same issue?'

'Yes, Behri. Everyone is upset that you took on a new person at a much higher salary than the existing guys.'

And that was that!

The Story of Mehringez

However, that is not the end of our story. Because I will now take you to another interview, this time conducted by Behringez's twin sister, Mehringez.

By a strange coincidence, even this interview proceeded in exactly the same way as the one you've just seen. Now, I could simply repeat what I had said earlier about Behringez and the interview she had conducted—and it would apply perfectly to Mehringez as well. In fact, I had a long and detailed discussion on this subject with my editor Radhika at Penguin Random House India. After all, if I were to repeat whole paragraphs several times in the book, it would increase the number of pages. Which, in turn, would allow us to charge more for the book. This was a truly tantalizing prospect, but finally, in the interest of ethics, we decided not to.

To summarize therefore, the candidate, Pankaj, was a great programmer and Mehringez was clear that she would take him on. But he also demanded a lakh a month as salary.

Like Behringez, Mehringez too almost jumped. 'A lakh a month? That's too high for a graduate with a couple of years of experience.'

As you might imagine, Pankaj was adamant. But this is where our second story takes a twist. 'Pankaj, you're a good programmer, and we would love to take you on,' said Mehringez. 'But in our company, we look after our people. If we give you a salary that is so much higher than that of our existing guys, we'd be very unfair to them, wouldn't we? By the same logic, if you were to join us and we were to take on someone with the same qualifications and experience as you, and pay him a higher salary, you'd be unhappy, wouldn't you? We'd definitely like you to join us, and we'll give you a decent salary. After that, it's up to you. Prove yourself, and you can rise rapidly. Does that sound okay?'

However, Pankaj was in no mood to listen. 'I'm sorry, ma'am, but that's the salary I'm looking for.'

And so, the two shook hands. The interview was over and Pankaj left.

The next day, Mehringez happened to overhear some of her colleagues chatting over lunch. And they were not aware that she could hear them.

'Mehri interviewed a very good programmer yesterday,' said one.

'So, was he selected?' was the natural query.

'No, his demands were too high. Mehri would never upset us by taking on someone from outside at a higher salary with the same experience.'

'Yes, I know. That's one big reason why we work with her. She looks after us and always gives us a fair deal. Which is why we trust her.'

And as you can guess, Mehringez smiled and walked on.

But hang on. You haven't heard the end of the story. As you might imagine, Pankaj got another job within days of his interview with Mehringez. A few months later, he was chatting with a friend. And he had a faraway look in his eyes. 'Yaar, I think I made a mistake. Maybe I should have joined Mehringez. Great boss to work for. She really looks after her people.'

And with that, my story about the twin sisters comes to an end. But for you, dear founder, it's just the beginning. Be fair to your people. Build trust in them. And you'll be able to build just the right team.

9

Build Your Team: The Story of Harry

Dear reader, you've now got your co-founder in place, and you've recruited the right people. But is that it?

Of course not. That's just the first step. You need to build this team. Develop your people. Help them grow. Motivate them so that they form just the RIGHT high-performance TEAM you need. In fact, I would take that a step further—everyone in the team should share in your dream. And hopefully stay with you longer than the few months that many youngsters stay in a company. Remember Sanjeev Bikhchandani's comment, 'Be a magnet for people. People don't work for companies. They work for people.' And you, dear founder must be that magnet. The reason why people would like to join your start-up.

While on this subject, one person who has always impressed me is my young friend Haribhai Founderbhai. A true DREAM Founder if ever I saw one. When I was writing this book, I was clear—this young man's story had to be told. His proud but conservative Gujarati parents had fondly named their son Haribhai. But when I spoke to him before writing this book, he was clear, 'Please call me Harry.' Of course, this was said when his parents were not around. Anyhow, in deference to his wishes, Harry is the name we will use.

Harry had created a start-up called Trainerbhai in the year 2014. A company in the business of conducting sales training programmes. And as you can see, his parents had had a more than minor role in the naming of the company. Organizations, both large and small, would send their sales force to Trainerbhai, and they would come back fully trained to meet—sorry—crack their sales targets. But that was not all. Trainerbhai had something unique going for it. You see, in any kind of training, you need constant follow-up to ensure that the skills learnt are not forgotten. Now, Harry realized this and therefore he had created a portal named Trainerbhai.com (what else?). People who had undergone the wonderful sales training programmes at Trainerbhai, would be able to come to this portal for regular updates, game-based learning, chat sessions and much more. In fact, the company was even experimenting with the use of machine learning to give advice to their participants.

Now, how they conducted their training programmes, and the subsequent follow-up, is not really of relevance to us here. What *is* relevant is the way Harry built his team. Phenomenal is not the word. His people loved him. They respected and trusted him. People who were not part of his company were desperate to join, simply to get a chance to work with Harry. In fact . . .

But once again, I'm getting ahead of myself. I have lots of stories about Harry, so let's start with the first one. A story about Farhaan (Furry for short), a sales professional with barely a couple of years of experience, who had applied to Trainerbhai for a job. Furry had heard a lot of stories about Harry, and the more he heard, the more impressed he was. He wanted to work with Harry and learn from him. So, let's join Furry as he trudged his way to the Trainerbhai office in Safdarjung Enclave, a colony in Delhi.

Furry reached the office a few minutes before the appointed time at 11 a.m. Actually, that's not strictly correct. Furry landed up at the address he had been given and looked around, perplexed.

The address was correct. But what he saw was a typical two-storey residential building. He had expected something else—perhaps a plush office of the kind that Accenture or KPMG might have had in Cyber City in Gurgaon. And he began to have second thoughts. Was this the kind of company he planned to join? But then he reasoned that this was a start-up, and perhaps his expectations were too high. Anyhow, since he had no option, he went in and spoke to the security guard on duty. The guard asked him who he wanted to meet, spoke briefly on the intercom, and then gruffly told Furry, '*Sahib abhi* busy *hain. Aap yahaan* wait *karo* (Sahib is busy right now. Wait here).'

This was, of course, completely expected. The founder of a company was a big man—even if the company was a start-up—and Furry sat down to wait in one of the plastic chairs available. He had met several senior people in life, and he realized he might have to wait for half an hour, perhaps even more. It was the done thing, you see. Senior people always kept you waiting, and if you had come for an interview, you could jolly well wait. Of course, if you didn't want to wait, you were welcome to leave. In any case, there were lots of candidates looking for a job—you were not the only one!

11 a.m. came and went. As Furry was idly flipping through the messages on his phone, he saw someone running down the staircase. 'Hi Furry, I'm Harry. I'm so sorry I'm late. Please come.' Saying which, the founder and CEO, Harry, escorted the young applicant, Furry, with just two years of experience, up the steps to his office.

Furry quickly checked his phone—it was 11.05 a.m. Just five minutes past the appointed time. And the CEO not only ran down the steps to personally escort him, but also apologized for being late. Five minutes late. And that too for a job applicant! As he went up the steps, Furry began to realize why Harry had such a terrific reputation in the world of start-ups.

When they reached the top floor, Furry looked around in surprise. Because in front of him was a two-room *barsaati*. Now I'm sure you've heard this term. If you haven't, let me add to your knowledge. A barsaati is a one-room or at the most a two-room apartment on the roof of a residential building. It's not a complete floor and has basically been created so that the landlord can get a little more rent. Usually, barsaatis are occupied by young bachelors who cannot afford anything better. But this one was occupied by the founder and CEO of Trainerbhai. As you can imagine, all Furry's misgivings came back with a bang. What kind of company was this? The CEO's office in a barsaati? Anyhow, having come all this way, Furry couldn't turn back, so he went in with Harry and sat down.

And the two of them started chatting. Harry spoke about his DREAM for the company. He mentioned the fact that the Indian industry was on the cusp of a huge growth phase and that companies needed good, trained salespersons. Lots and lots of them. And therefore, sales training was the need of the hour. No, it was the need of the decade, or even the century. And of course, it had to be combined with comprehensive follow-up. Which had to be done digitally so that salespersons could access it from wherever they were. And that no other company was focusing on these two as a package. And, of course, the fact that Trainerbhai planned to become a leader in this space, not just in India, but across the world as well . . .

Now, while Harry was speaking, you should have seen Furry's face. Yes sir, slowly but steadily, Furry started believing in Harry's dream. Such was Harry's passion. His conviction. Furry realized that Harry was not running a business—he was chasing his dream. And when Furry finally left the office, he did not see a miserable, puny start-up. He did not see a barsaati any more. He saw the office of the CEO of a future multinational. One that was well on its way to becoming a world leader in sales training.

On the way out, he happened to meet some of the youngsters who already worked there. 'Harry is cool, man, real cool,' said a long-haired programmer with a straggly beard who appeared to be smoking his umpteenth cigarette of the day. And then he got friendly. 'All bosses are demanding, and so is he. But he doesn't expect you to do anything that he himself doesn't do. Let me tell you a story. Harry is very finicky about deadlines. If you've got a deadline, brother, you've got to meet it. Once, as part of a project, we had set Harry a deadline. This was at a time when he was really busy. But he stayed awake all night, worked on his task, and walked into the office bleary-eyed after a night of zero sleep. But—and this is the amazing part—he met the deadline, even though he hadn't slept at all. He really leads by example, and doesn't expect us to do anything that he himself wouldn't do. Great boss.'

And what do you think Furry did? All his doubts put to rest, he went through with the rest of the recruitment process, hoping against hope that he would be selected. Fortunately, he was. And the moment that happened, he decided to join. When he got interview calls from the other, much larger companies he had applied to, he didn't even attend the interviews. Instead, he politely told them that he was withdrawing his application. Of course, you can guess the rest. Furry joined almost immediately, and he's still there. And oh, I must share with you a conversation that Furry had with a bunch of friends in a bar that night (where else?). 'My God, that guy is just too much. *He came down personally to meet me*. He didn't phone up the security guard and ask him to send me up. No, he actually came down. And you know, he apologized for being five minutes late. *Bhai, paanch* minute *kya cheez hai* (what are five minutes)? Harry really respects people. And he leads by example. If he expects something from you, he expects it from himself as well . . .'

With that, Furry took a lo-o-o-ng swig of his beer, as he continued, 'The other thing is that the guy really believes in his dream. And you know what? You spend ten minutes with him, and you start believing in it as well. Folks, I am very, very clear. This is where I'm going to work!'

Communicate, Communicate, Communicate

So, Furry joined Trainerbhai. And over time, he realized that Harry shared something with all great leaders—he believed in communication. Every room in the office (remember, this was a residential building with bedrooms and drawing rooms) had a prominently displayed poster, titled, 'Our Dream'. Every Monday, they would have a meeting which all the staff would attend. That's right, I said all the staff, not just the senior guys. Starting with the juniormost intern. Where they would discuss everything that had happened during the past week and plan for the next one. Almost from day one, Furry began to feel he was part of the organization. He knew what was happening, who was doing what, which orders had been lost, and who the competitors were. Yes sir, Furry was not just another employee. He was a part of the organization.

But one day, it had to happen. As you are aware, in November 2016, the government of India demonetized high-value currency notes. Now, I do not want to get into the pros and cons of this decision (perhaps I will, in another book), but I must tell you the impact it had on Trainerbhai. You see, many of their clients were small companies that would send one or two sales guys at a time to attend the training programmes. Many of these companies used to deal in cash. But now there was no cash, so their business plummeted. And when your business plummets, what's the first thing on your mind? Survival, of course. And what's the last thing? Training!

So that's what happened to Trainerbhai—at least for a few months. Many of their smaller clients stopped sending people to be trained, and business came down to rock bottom. Tough times. And employees became more and more nervous. 'Will the company survive this crisis?' 'What costs will they cut?' Most important, 'Will I be asked to leave?' You see? Everyone in Trainerbhai was jittery about the company and, even more important, about his or her job.

And what do you think Harry did? Did he shut himself up in his office, drinking cup after cup of coffee, worrying himself sick and refusing to talk to anyone? No, my friend. This was not the Harry I knew. He realized that his team of young men and women was desperately concerned. They wanted to talk to him. They wanted to know what was going on. They wanted to feel that the company would be able to ride out the crisis. And that's exactly what he did. Soon after demonetization, he organized a meeting with all his people where he shared everything that was happening. Yes, he was completely transparent. People were made aware of the problems the company was facing. He also took their opinions on possible solutions to tide over the crisis. Most of all, he told his people that no one would lose his or her job. In fact, even salaries would not be reduced, unless the company was forced into a corner. For the moment, salaries continued.

And what do you think his people felt? Relief, of course! They all knew there was a problem, but they wanted to hear it from the horse's mouth. And the fact that Harry was taking their opinion on managing during those tough times really helped. Because it made them truly feel they were part of the organization. They trusted Harry. In fact, it wouldn't be wrong to say that this was the time the entire team of Trainerbhai really became one solid unit.

Harry kept up this communication every week, right through the crisis. And then slowly the dust began to settle, and business began to look up. And the company emerged far stronger from the crisis. Business began to boom again. But most of all, Harry was able to retain all his people. Simply because he believed in communicating with his team!

So now you've met my young friend Harry. And you've seen why he is able to motivate his team and get them to perform. Because he has respect for each of them. Because he is passionate and is able to share this passion with them. Because he leads by example. And, of course, because he communicates, communicates and communicates!

Now, before I end, I simply have to tell you something that Harry once told me. Over chai and samosas, of course. 'I don't offer people a job. No, that's too ordinary. I tell them that if they want a job, they should go elsewhere. I offer them a dream. And they should join me only if they share in this dream. But once they do join me, well, I promise them one thing. I promise them we would have a great time chasing our dream together . . .'

10

Develop Your People

Let me tell you another story about Haribhai—sorry, Harry—and how he built his team. One fine day, Harry hired a salesperson called Carishma. At least that's what her parents had named her. But you know how young people are, don't you? She preferred the name Carrie, and in deference to her wishes, that's what we'll call her in this story. Carrie did have a couple of years of experience before joining the company, but that's about all. Of course, she was willing to learn and that was the main thing.

Now, as the CEO of the company, Harry was naturally its star salesperson as well. He would make all important presentations. Carrie would make the sales calls and fix up the presentations. She would also help in making the PowerPoint presentations. But—and I will repeat this—the actual presentations were critical to the company, so Harry made them.

However, one day Harry called Carrie to his barsaati. 'Carrie, you've just fixed up a presentation with the CEO of Maddy Industries. I think you should make this presentation.'

Carrie stared goggle-eyed at Harry. 'Me? Presentation? To the CEO?'

'Yes, why not? You understand our business by now. And I'm sure you'll be able to make it. Any problems?'

'N-n-no, Harry. N-no, I don't think so.'

'Don't worry. I'll come along with you and sit through it. But you handle the presentation.'

Saying which, Harry smiled at her. The discussion was over, and Carrie left in a bit of a daze. 'Presentation to a CEO? Admittedly it is not one of our major clients. But a CEO? I've never done it in my life. My god . . .' And she walked over to the coffee machine, poured herself a stiff one and sat down at her desk, wondering what to do.

Dear reader, I now want you to guess what happened next. That's right. The presentation was three days away, and for those three days Carrie slogged night and day. Even her boyfriend began to wonder what he had done wrong, because she barely spoke to him. And even when she did, she was preoccupied. She created the presentation, junked it, created it again, junked it again, and again, till at last she was satisfied. And then, of course, she practised making the presentation to a live audience (her dog, in case you hadn't guessed). Fortunately, the dog had no objections, and wagged his tail every time she asked for his opinion.

And then, the big day arrived. Fortified with two extra eggs for breakfast—just to give her confidence—Carrie reached the office. And together, she and Harry left for the client meeting. The presentation itself went off fairly well. Not brilliant, you see, but decent. The client was reasonably happy. Harry tackled most of the questions, but the presentation itself was entirely Carrie's. Once they were back, Harry asked her what she had learnt and what she could do to improve it. Carrie already had her answers ready, and she told him.

'Great,' said Harry. We have another one coming up this Friday with Balto Industries. You make this one again.'

This time, the butterflies in Carrie's stomach were slightly more restful. But once again, she prepared round the clock. Once again, the poor dog was subjected to something he had no clue about. And once again, Carrie made the presentation with Harry tackling most of the questions. Most, not all. Because by now, Carrie was able to tackle some of them, you see.

I don't think I need to tell you what happened next. That's right, Harry kept giving Carrie opportunity after opportunity. And with her basic intelligence and diligence, she kept improving every time. Till one fine day when Harry told her, 'Carrie, I'm busy all of this week. I can't join you. Why don't you make the presentation to Ralco yourself?' And, of course, Carrie beamed at him. 'Sure, boss. I'll do it.'

Now, I'm sure you can figure out what Harry was trying to do. That's right, he was trying to develop Carrie into a person who could tackle senior clients on her own. By giving her opportunities and at the same time, discussing with her how she could improve. You see, he was a true believer in empowering his people. And, of course, Carrie responded—nervously at first, but delightedly later. As you might imagine, she became a star salesperson for Trainerbhai.

By the way, several clients offered her a job. With more money. But did she leave? No, my friend, she stayed on with Trainerbhai and with Harry. Because Harry had helped her to learn and to grow. And continued to do so. And, by the way, this wasn't true for Carrie alone. Harry's whole style of management was such. He would identify people who had potential, develop them, and ultimately empower them. No micromanagement for him. And for this, his team looked up to him and refused to leave the organization.

Yes sir, if you really want to develop and motivate your team, do learn from Harry. Everyone wants to keep learning and growing. Give them responsibility. Empower them. Help them to learn and to grow. And you'll be surprised how great a team you can build.

Just the way Harry did!

11

Treat Them like Your Family

Now that you've met our young friend Harry, you've seen how he developed his team. But there is one more thing I must tell you. He would treat them like his family. True, he was a busy, busy man. He barely had time to think, let alone eat. In his office at 8 a.m. sharp, he would swing into action well before even the office boy landed up. Yes sir, Harry always worked at a frenetic pace, which is why his company was doing well. But he never, ever forgot his team.

Want to know more? Okay, here are four stories about Harry and his team . . .

Story 1: The Unhappy Programmer

A couple of years after its launch, there was one problem that the Trainerbhai.com portal faced, and that too, consistently. There seemed to be a bug in the software. Users would get logged out, apparently at random. And they would need to log in once again. The worrying part of course, was that this happened with monotonous regularity, and feedback was dipping. A real problem, you see, because there were competitors lurking around just waiting to snatch away their clients. And that explains why Harry was highly tense and worked up. The problem had been festering for some time and simply refused to get resolved.

Now, Harry had an interesting habit that he had developed over the years. He called it 'management by floating around'. He would pick up a cup of coffee and simply wander around the office. Noticing what was going on, talking to people here and there, pepping up the odd person who looked downcast . . .

And that is when he noticed Jerry. Now Jerry was one of the crack software developers in the team. Whenever the other programmers were stuck, they would come to him for advice. And he would never let them down. If you are aware of the software industry, he was popularly known as a cat programmer. But today, he did not look like a cat programmer at all. No sir. Bent over his desk, with his head in his hands, he looked the picture of misery. Perhaps even more.

And that's what Harry noticed. He stopped and put a friendly hand on Jerry's shoulder. 'What's up, Jerry?' he asked, although he knew what Jerry's problem was. You see, Jerry lived with his father. Unfortunately, relations between the two were far from pleasant. In fact, they were downright antagonistic—not too different from the relations between India and Pakistan on the Line of Control. But today, Jerry appeared even more downcast than usual. And when he looked up, he appeared tired and defeated. Definitely not how a bright, young twenty-six-year-old should look.

'Nothing, boss,' he managed to blurt out.

But, of course, the boss was Harry, and he sensed trouble. 'Come, Jerry, let's go out.'

And so, Harry and Jerry went out of the office, down the steps and across the road to Bengal Sweet House. The 'Welcomgroup Sheraton' of Trainerbhai, if you know what I mean. Where all the youngsters would land up when they wanted a break. Or wanted to chit-chat about their girlfriends. Or boyfriends. And have a coke or a chai, depending on the current state of their usually precarious financial position. So, Harry and Jerry entered Bengal Sweet House and took a table in the dingiest, dirtiest corner, where they would not be disturbed.

'*Kya baat hai,* Jerry (What happened)?' asked Harry, after the rasgullas and coke had been ordered. But Jerry wouldn't speak. Head down, looking the picture of dejection, he simply sat quietly, taking a sip of his coke from time to time. So, Harry sat there, waiting patiently. And over the second plate of rasgullas (they were both young men, you see), Jerry opened up. Gradually at first, but ultimately in a torrent. Apparently, his father objected strongly to his girlfriend (the current one—remember, this was a young man in the twenty-first century). In fact, they had had a showdown in the morning, just before Jerry left for office. And perhaps for the first time in his life, Jerry was utterly defeated. Morale down, brain not really functioning, simply waiting for life to give him whatever knocks it had in store.

And what about Harry? Did he play counsellor? Did he give precious words of advice that Jerry could put into practice? No sir. All Harry did was to listen to him. Quietly, patiently, without hurrying him up. He let Jerry open up and share his problems. You see, no one can solve anyone else's personal problems. But what you *can* do is to listen patiently. And empathize. Genuinely empathize. Sometimes that's all a human being needs—another human being who is willing to listen. Without broadcasting it to all and sundry, of course.

Over the third plate of rasgullas and the second coke, Jerry began to perk up. He had shared his problem with someone. The problem had not been solved. No way. But he had got it off his chest, and that itself was half the solution. It was a visibly perked-up Jerry who then made a statement that Harry was to remember for the rest of his life, 'Harry, I'll do anything for you!'

And now, dear reader, I have some good news for you. Jerry was not part of the team that was working on the problem of users getting logged out. But on his own, he joined the team, worked three nights in a row—snatching a few hours of sleep when he could—and managed to solve the problem. The office was delighted, and Jerry became a hero. And they all trooped into

Bengal Sweet House to celebrate. Not in the dingiest, darkest corner. No way. This time, they were in the brightest, most garish, noisiest area. Wolfing down—what else—rasgullas, of course!

Story 2: The Angry Salesperson

One of Harry's salespersons was called Barry (I'm not too sure what his real name was, so we'll let that pass). Anyhow, Barry was good at his job. He was diligent, he followed up with his clients methodically, and his relations with them were fine. Well, not always, but most of the time.

You see, Barry was a highly stressed-out person by nature. You know what I mean, of course. And he would often get angry. No, that's too mild a term—he would erupt like a volcano. Of course, once the lava was out, he would calm down, but the explosion would have happened by then. And that got him into scraps from time to time.

So now you know enough about Barry. And you can imagine why, on that fateful Wednesday afternoon, he walked into office looking like a volcano that had decided to erupt. Or perhaps a pressure cooker that was constantly blowing off steam. He went to his seat and sat down, not even bothering to look around. Someone brought him coffee, which he barely acknowledged, as he sat glaring at the world around him.

At that moment, Harry just happened to walk across to his table. And saw Barry in his current state of absolute peace.

'What happened, Barry?' he asked.

Barry simply glared at the poor wastepaper basket without answering.

Now, Harry was young, but he was smart. He realized what was happening. '*Chal*, coffee *peetey hain* (Come, let's have a cup of coffee)'. Saying which, he took Barry by the arm and dragged him to the coffee machine. And there, of course, the whole story came out. Barry had a client called Gusseywala, who was exactly that. He was arrogant, obnoxious, cynical . . . in fact, you can add any similar adjectives and they would fit him to a nicety. Now apparently, this gentleman—if you could call him that—had called Barry a liar to his face. But, believe me, Barry was not a liar. It could have been a misunderstanding that led to this term being thrown at him, but he was most definitely not a liar. Quite naturally, he had reacted, and that too angrily. After a few heated exchanges, he had stormed out of Gusseywala's office. And that is how we found him half an hour later.

Obviously, Harry sympathized with Barry. But that was not the end. Because he then said, 'Barry, a few of us are getting together for dinner at the Casanova Bar tonight. Why don't you join us, say, at eight?'

Barry grudgingly agreed, and 8 p.m. found him entering the Casanova Bar. A close observer would have noticed that the volcano was somewhat calmer than it had been in the afternoon. Anyhow, he walked in and saw Harry and his girlfriend, along with a very close friend and *his* girlfriend. That's it. Just the four of them, and Barry. Over drinks and dinner, Barry realized that it was Harry's girlfriend's birthday and that's why the four of them had come out to celebrate.

Suddenly, it hit Barry like a hammer. Harry had realized that Barry was upset—very upset. He also knew that Barry lived alone, away from his parents who were in a different town. Harry did not want Barry to spend the evening alone, brooding. And that's why he had invited him to this highly private birthday celebration.

Harry's gesture was deeply moving and touching, and Barry was deeply moved and touched. 'What a boss. He has a private birthday get-together for his girlfriend, with just two more close friends invited. And he invited me, simply because I was upset, and he didn't want to leave me alone.'

And Barry shook his head in admiration, 'I'll do anything for him. What a boss!'

Story 3: The Programmer Who Left

You've already seen how Harry treated people who were part of his team. But hang on. What about people who used to work with him, but had now resigned and left Trainerbhai? Wouldn't you like to know how he treated them? So, let's take a peep at Orry, one of the better programmers in the company. Orry had been with Trainerbhai for a couple of years and had done well. He had contributed significantly to the Trainerbhai.com portal that the company had developed. But, as you are aware, young people are restless. Unlike their fathers—or perhaps grandfathers—they do not hang on to one employer till they retire. They move on. And therefore, after two great years at Trainerbhai, Orry felt that he needed to shift to the exciting new field of virtual reality. Unfortunately, that was not possible within Trainerbhai, so Orry had to quit and shift to another company.

Now, like everything else at Trainerbhai, the parting was happy. There was the usual party, with pastries and samosas and backslapping and soppy speeches. The kind that are inevitably made whenever someone leaves. And, of course, the farewell gift. Party over, Orry hugged his colleagues (this was before Covid times and hugging was the done thing) and left. And life returned to normal.

There is, however, one important thing that I want you to notice. Every time Trainerbhai had a get-together—usually at a bar—Orry was invited. Even though he had left. So were all the other people who had left the company. Now, I could describe each one of these people in great detail, but please remember this story is about Orry, so let's focus on him. Of course, Orry invariably attended these get-togethers. He wasn't an employee any more, but if you were to check the attendance records at these parties, he was one of the most regular attendees. In fact, at times, he would drop in to the Trainerbhai office in the evening just to chill and relive old times. It was as though he hadn't really left.

However, this is where our happy story takes a bit of a twist. One day, Orry landed up at Trainerbhai and met Harry. Now, if you had happened to be there and had seen his face, you would have realized that there was something wrong. And you would have been absolutely right. Like many start-ups, Orry's current employer had shut shop. And Orry was without a job. With retired parents to take care of. And that explains the meeting between Orry and Harry. QED.

Orry blurted out his problem. 'Harry, I'm very happy in the field of virtual reality, so I'm looking for a possible opening within this field. I know that Trainerbhai is not into virtual reality at all, otherwise I would have come right back to you. I've applied to a few places, but it'll take time. Don't know how much time, but I have to earn in the meantime.' And having said that, Orry took a glum sip of his coffee. Which, in keeping with the general mood, had turned cold.

Now, I want you to watch carefully what Harry did. He walked across the table, sat next to Orry and gave him a big hug. 'Orry, you will always be a part of our team. This is your home. You are always welcome back—even if it is for a couple of months. We do have a project that needs your help. Let's get started. And don't worry about money—we'll take care of you. More coffee?'

And you should have seen Orry's reaction. He looked as though he was about to kiss Harry. Fortunately, that didn't happen, otherwise my story might have had a different ending. But he did everything except that. Beaming, with a steaming mug of coffee in front of him, Orry rolled up his sleeves and sank his teeth into the project Harry had mentioned.

Of course, he was good. Very good. Within a couple of months, he got another job in the area of virtual reality, which he accepted. But he told his new employer that he needed to finish what he was doing at Trainerbhai, and would therefore need another fifteen days to join. So, Orry finished the project and then shifted.

But that is still not the end of the story. Every time Harry wanted help in tackling a ticklish technical problem, Orry was available. Obviously, he could not come over during the day. He would work nights, sometimes carrying his toothbrush to Trainerbhai's office. But he would never say no.

By the way, was this a story about Orry? No, my friend, it was also a story about Ranga. And Gurmeet. And Sofia. And Satinder . . .

In fact, it wasn't a story about any of these former employees of Trainerbhai. Yes, you've guessed right. It was a story about Harry! And how he built a family. Where ex-employees were as welcome as employees.

And if you are creating a start-up, I'm sure you would want to learn from Harry, wouldn't you?

Story 4: The Marriage Counsellor

This is the fourth, and perhaps the most fascinating story of all. And for this one, I need to introduce you to two more members of Harry's team, namely Punjab Singh and Annie Cochin Jacob. Good people, both of them. And very good workers—Harry had told me so. So, why do I want to talk about them? Well, for a start, they came from two different states of India—which is evident from their names. Punjab Singh came from Punjab. Where else? And Annie came from Kerala.

'So what?' you're probably thinking. 'People can come from any state in India. There's no law against it.'

Okay, so let me take it further. Punjab Singh was a Sikh, and Annie was a Christian. Now, can you figure out why I've introduced them?

No? Okay, one more hint. These two young people wanted to get married.

Still not clear? After all, people from different backgrounds and different religions do get married.

Okay, since you still haven't guessed, let me give you the full picture. All four parents were dead against the match. Annie's parents wanted her to marry a nice Keralite Christian boy, and Punjab's parents wanted him to marry a nice Sikh girl. Other than the fact that both sets of parents wanted someone 'nice', there was absolutely nothing else in common.

'Aha! Why didn't you tell me this earlier?'

Well, I wanted you to guess.

'But what does this have to do with this book?'

Everything. You see, one day when Harry was floating around his office, he realized that something was wrong. Like all good bosses, he was aware of the personal lives of his team members. He knew that these two youngsters were keen to get married. But of late, both of them had become a bit irritable, and each used to spend time staring into space with a somewhat vacant expression.

Again, like all good bosses, Harry was concerned. So, he took Punjab to the local counselling centre, Bengal Sweet House (where else?). Having ordered the usual fare of samosas and coke, he asked the younger man, 'What's the matter, Punjab? You seem to be very preoccupied.'

Punjab's mouth was full of a partially eaten samosa, so he took a while to speak. Even after that, he hemmed and hawed and wouldn't open up. It took two more samosas and one more bottle of coke to get him to talk. 'Boss, it's me and Annie.'

'Yes, I know. I've known for some time. But what's the issue?'

Punjab thought for a moment. 'Boss, we want to get married.'

'That's great. Congrats,' said Harry as he put out his hand.

Punjab shook his hand absent-mindedly and thought for a moment. 'No boss, there is an issue. We are keen to get married, but our parents are against it.'

And that's when it became clear to Harry. He watched Punjab in action devouring yet another samosa—which was actually quite an entertaining sight. After a minute, he came to a decision.

'Punjab, we are like a family. And when a member of a family is in trouble, the others rally around to help him. Are you okay with me helping out?'

Punjab stared at Harry. 'You? How can you help? You don't even know our parents.'

'True. But I might be able to suggest a way to tackle them. Tell you what. Talk to Annie, and if she's okay, the three of us can have a chat.'

And with that, the two of them left Bengal Sweet House and went back to the office. However, within half an hour, Punjab walked over to Harry's desk. 'Boss, I've spoken to Annie, and she's fine with the idea.'

'Great. I have a meeting till 6 p.m. Let's stroll down to our old friend, Bengal Sweet House, at six.'

And so, shortly after 6 p.m. the three of them could be seen sitting at one of the hallowed tables of Bengal Sweet House. As usual, Punjab had two hefty samosas in front of him, along with the mandatory coke. Annie, who was a bit more figure-conscious, had a diet coke. For the next hour, the three of them debated, strategized, ideated, and did whatever else they could, to come up with a plan to convince the four parents. Several options were discussed and discarded, but at last they were able to arrive at what they thought had a chance of working. And with a last sip of the coke as well as the diet coke (depending on who was taking the sip), the three of them crept back to office.

What was the strategy these guys had worked out? I don't know. In fact, it doesn't really matter, because this is a story about building teams and not about marriages. The important thing is what I heard Punjab and Annie discussing just before they took an auto home that night. Yes, that's right, I happened to be right there when they were waiting for an auto. 'What a guy,' gushed Punjab. 'He spent an hour with us just figuring out how to convince our parents. What a guy!' And, of course, Annie's comments were no different, 'Great guy. That's one big reason why we all love to work with him!'

And that, my friend, is why I told you this story about Harry. By the way, don't get me wrong. As the captain of the ship, you do not need to become a marriage counsellor. Don't be silly—you have a business to run, don't you? But you must be concerned. That's what your people are looking forward to. Concern and empathy. After all, a great team should feel like a family, shouldn't it?

Of course, I must tell you what finally happened. Punjab and Annie did get married. And they were obviously delighted. So were their parents. As was Harry, because he had been able to help.

But there was one more person who was delighted.

Who?

Come on—the owner of Bengal Sweet House, of course. For him, Harry was a major account, given the number of meetings he held there. Every time Harry walked in, the owner would give him a beaming smile and a namaste! In fact, he once told me that he was looking forward to more bosses like Harry sir!

So that was Harry and his team.

No, let me correct myself—that was Harry and his family!

12

But Don't Take Any Nonsense

Dear founder, in these last few chapters, you've met our wonderful young leader, Harry, and seen how he built an equally wonderful team.

But hang on. Life cannot always be hunky-dory, can it? What if some people do not respond to all this positivity? What if they take undue advantage? What if they do not conform to what is expected of them? What if—unfortunately—there are a few rotten apples in the lot? Would DREAM Founders like Harry still mollycoddle them? Would they happily be taken for a ride?

Of course not! Building a great team does not mean you get taken for granted. It doesn't mean people can do exactly as they please. DREAM Founders like Harry are tough guys, and they know how to handle such people. So, let's watch Harry tackle some such people. In fact, three such people . . .

Story 1: When Harry Met Sally

Our friend Harry had just given out annual increments. Some of his employees were happy. Some were non-committal. A few were unhappy, and the most unhappy of the lot was Sally. A very good programmer, Sally believed the company was being grossly unfair to her. She was clear that she should have got at least 20 per cent more. In fact, she was convinced that she could get even more if she were to leave her job and look around. After all, Python programmers were not easy to find, were they?

Anyhow, after getting the news, Sally had rushed to the coffee vending machine to sulk. For precisely half an hour. That half an hour and the hot coffee helped her to make up her mind. She barged into Harry's room (the barsaati, remember?) where he was holding a meeting, and insisted on speaking to him. Naturally, Harry was a bit surprised at the vehemence in her tone, but he realized something was wrong. So, he quickly wound up his meeting and asked her to come in.

'Harry, the increment you have given me is grossly unfair. I'm worth much more. If you don't raise it significantly, I quit.' And with that she glared at him and walked out.

Dear reader, if you've been reading this book carefully, I'm sure you are thinking, 'This situation sounds familiar. I've seen it somewhere before.' If you don't, you've probably been sleeping, so please go right back and read the story about Mehringez and Behringez in chapter 8. I refuse to repeat myself. Now, the situation that Harry faced was fairly similar, except that it was an existing employee rather than an external candidate demanding a higher salary. And like Mehringez, Harry was smart as well, so you would not expect him to give in to this kind of blackmail either. Yes sir, that's exactly what it was. 'Give me a raise, or I'll quit'. If that isn't blackmail, I don't know what is.

On the other hand, he couldn't afford to lose Sally, especially so soon after losing another good programmer, Pytho. That was his dilemma.

Now, over time, Harry had figured out a way to react to situations like this. He would go down the steps of his office and take off for a quiet walk—as quiet as possible in the daytime in Delhi. Freed from the constant phone calls and interruptions, he found that this helped him think. And that's exactly what he did.

Ten minutes later, he was back. Decision made. He walked up to Sally and took her along to the coffee machine in the office where both of them picked up steaming cups of coffee. And then they went into his office, the barsaati.

'Sally, let's go back to what happened half an hour ago,' began Harry. 'First of all, I must tell you that I understand your point of view. You feel that you are a very good programmer, and I agree wholeheartedly. You also feel you need to be paid more. Looking at it from your point of view, that sounds fair.

However, just for a moment, look at my point of view.'

Sally glared at him, but a keen observer would have noticed that she was a bit less belligerent. 'OK. Tell me.'

'You see, Sally, I need to run this company. And I have a problem. I cannot be seen to be giving in to anyone who holds a gun to my head. I'm sorry, you may not like this, but when you say you'll quit if you don't get a raise immediately, you are holding a gun to my head.'

Now, dear reader, I want you to notice something very, very important here. Perhaps shut the book, go for a walk like Harry, and think. And maybe fold the page as a bookmark. You see, Harry never used the word blackmail. No way. That would have made Sally hit the ceiling. Wouldn't you, if your boss told you that you were blackmailing him? So the word blackmail was out!

Anyhow, Harry continued, 'Sally, let me suggest something. Take the rest of the day off. Think about what I've just said. Come back tomorrow. Please, please, don't hold a gun to my head, and we can talk.' At this point, Harry laughed—and, by the way, that laugh actually eased the tension in the room. Even Sally smiled for the first time.

So, the next morning saw Harry and Sally sitting across the table, with the inevitable cups of coffee between them. Sally was still clear that she wanted a raise, but a close observer would have noticed that her belligerence was gone and she actually looked more peaceful.

'So Sally, I hope you've removed the gun that you were holding to my head,' started off Harry.

'Yes,' was the response, and it was a calmer response. 'But I still believe I deserve more.'

'Great,' said Harry and he smiled. 'Now I need to share two things with you. First of all, you are definitely a very good programmer. And an asset to our company. And when you say you should be earning more, I see your point. Whether I agree with that or not—I'll come to that a bit later.'

'You see Sally, as the CEO, I need to run this company. For a moment, put yourself in my shoes. If I were to give you a raise right now, you know what would happen, don't you?'

'Yes, everyone else will demand a raise.'

'Absolutely. And that's not good for the company. Because then, every time someone is unhappy with his salary, his role, his designation, or anything else, all he would need to do is walk into this room and threaten to quit if his demands were not met. Because I would have set a precedent with you. And no one forgets precedents. You see?'

'Yes, I do,' said Sally, wondering what was coming. *Was this the end of the raise?*

'Fine. By the way, I would like to give you a raise, but it cannot be linked to what happened yesterday. Because then we are sending a clear message, "Threaten the boss, and he'll give in".'

Once again, Sally nodded.

'Now, there's one very important thing I want to know from you. I would like to do something about the issue you have raised, but you'll have to give me a bit of time. Can you leave the problem with me? Can you trust me?'

Sally thought for a moment. What Harry was saying made sense. She realized that he could not give in to her demands right away. And he had always been a fair boss. Making up her mind, she blurted out, 'Okay'.

At this, Harry took a deep breath. The crisis was over for the moment. Of course, the problem still had to be solved, but at least he had taken care of the blackmail issue.

Now, what do you think Harry did? Well, he was smart, so he figured out a way. Sally and another colleague called Vally—actually Vallabh—were working on an extension to the Trainerbhai.com portal. And this project was likely to get over in a couple of months. The day that happened and the portal went live, Harry called Sally into his room again, 'Sally, that was a great job. And from next month, I'm increasing your salary by 15 per cent!'

Sally beamed at Harry. 'Thank you, Harry. You've made my day.' And she walked out of the room happily.

But that was not all. Harry called in Vally, the other programmer who had worked on the project. 'Vally, that was a great job. And I'm increasing your salary from next month.'

'Wow, thanks boss,' said Vally. He had never even expected this raise and gave Harry a huge grin.

A few days later, Harry happened to meet his twin brother, Parry, who was also running a start-up (yes, even I have been amazed at the number of twins I've met while writing this book). They met at a pub, naturally. Over beer and dhokla, Harry shared with his brother what had happened. Of course, Parry acknowledged the smart way in which Harry had resolved the issue. But he did have two questions. 'Harry, I can understand what you did, and I think it was the right decision. But what if it did not work? What if Sally had quit?'

Harry nodded, 'You're right, Parry. In fact, I have faced one such situation where my approach did not work, and the employee left. A good employee. But I still believe I took the right decision. Can't give in to blackmail. Can't set a bad precedent, because that will hound you forever.'

'Yes, I see your point,' said Parry. However, he had not finished yet. 'Everything sounds fine. But there's one thing I haven't understood. Why did you give a mid-year raise to Vally? He never asked for it, did he?'

Harry had a smug expression on his face as he asked for a refill of his beer. 'Yes, that was a masterstroke, wasn't it? I realized that if I had only given a raise to Sally, it would have sent the wrong message once again. Everyone in the office would still believe that I had given in to her demands. But by giving both Sally and Vally a raise, I linked the raise to the successful completion of the project, and not to Sally's gun. And anyway, both are great employees.'

This made eminent sense, and Parry nodded. But there was someone else who nodded.

The bearded professor, who was sitting at the next table, turned around. 'Well done, Harry. Those were good decisions.' And with that, he raised his mug of beer as the three of them clinked their mugs.

'Cheers!'

Story 2: The Case of the Inflated Bills

One of Harry's star salespersons was a young man named Jolly. And Harry was happy with him. So all was well, you might think. But no. All was not well. You see, Jolly had a habit of inflating the expenses he claimed. The company allowed employees to claim expenses that were incurred for official purposes, such as local conveyance by auto. And Jolly's claims were invariably exaggerated. As an example, for a trip that would usually cost Rs 100, Jolly would claim anywhere between Rs 150 and Rs 200. Harry knew he was being fooled. And he hated it. But he didn't want to lose a good sales guy, so he kept quiet. And in the process, the habit obviously grew.

Not only that, Harry realized that the disease was spreading. Jolly had a habit of bragging to his colleagues, and often Harry would hear him at the coffee machine boasting to his colleagues how he used to increase his earnings. Quite naturally, the others also picked up these 'best practices' and started inflating their claims as well. It was most frustrating, but Harry simply didn't know what to do. He didn't want to confront Jolly and lose a good sales guy—anyway, it wasn't too easy to get such people. But this was simply not acceptable. The problem had to be solved. The only issue was *how*? Harry was at his wits' end, and often spent the day brooding over the problem. Even in the evening, his usual chilled beer appeared flat—almost like a medicine.

One evening, he was attending a webinar conducted by his mentor, the bearded professor. Suddenly he was galvanized into action, and almost spilt his beer on to his trousers. Something the professor had said hit him hard. He couldn't wait to get back to office the next day, and in his excitement, landed up even earlier than usual. That day, Jolly submitted his local conveyance form as always. With the usual smirk of course, which seemed to say, 'The boss never comes to know.' But this time was different. No sir, this time was very, very different. Harry called Jolly into his room and put a friendly arm across his shoulder. 'Jolly yaar, all of us need to be careful. Most of these auto drivers have doctored their meters. And they run fast. We need to be aware of the charges from, say, Lajpat Nagar to Connaught Place (these are two prominent locations in Delhi, in case you didn't know). As you can see, this guy has solidly overcharged you.' And Harry pointed to the offending entry in the local conveyance form. 'Not your fault, of course, but you need to be aware of what the correct charges should be.'

Jolly didn't know what to say. But, of course, he nodded. 'Yes, boss, you could be right.' And it was a somewhat chastened young man who let himself out of Harry's room.

What had the professor said, that had changed Harry's thinking? Very simple. 'Your purpose is not to find fault with your employee. If you confront him and tell him he is fudging bills, you are hitting his ego. No one likes to be called a crook. And, in the process, you would either force him to quit, or perhaps worse, you have a sullen employee on your hands. Definitely less productive than before.

'Remember, your objective is not to tell him he is a crook. Your objective is to let him know that you are aware of the inflated bills. People are smart. They get the message. If the boss is aware of the fudging, the chances are that they will cut it down, if not knock it out altogether.' And that was the miraculous piece of advice Harry had got from his mentor.

So that ends our interesting story. Well, not quite—there is a bit more, so do read on. That afternoon, when Harry went to the coffee machine to pick up his usual cup, he just happened to overhear Jolly speaking to two colleagues. '*Boss ko pata lag gaya hai* (The boss has come to know).' Of course, they didn't know that the boss had heard. And he wouldn't tell them that he had heard. No sir. Job done, he filled up his mug with steaming coffee and went back to his room with a smile.

Story 3: The Case of the Overwritten Bills

And now, let me tell you another story about Harry and the bills. Harry had another employee called Imaandar Kumar, or Imaan for short. This gentleman was responsible for the administration of the office—things like purchases, maintenance, cleanliness, etc. He was good at his work, but for some reason, Harry felt he could not trust him. Why? He couldn't put a finger on the reason, but there was a vague misgiving somewhere at the back of his mind. Anyhow, life carried on . . .

As I've mentioned, part of Imaan's job was purchases. And once he had purchased something for the office, he would submit the bill to Harry for approval. One day, Harry found a bill waiting for him. But this was no ordinary bill. It was clear that in the price column an amount of Rs 350 had been changed to Rs 850. Simple overwriting!

Now, this was completely unacceptable. Fortunately, Harry knew this particular supplier, so he called him up and checked the price of this item. And he was right. The figure should have been Rs 350. Imaan had modified the figure to increase the amount he had claimed.

Now, this was the first time Harry had faced such a situation. And he didn't know what to do. So he stepped out of the office to think. Should he confront Imaan? Or should he give him the benefit of doubt, as he had done with Jolly in the earlier story? Harry's mind was in turmoil, and he realized only one person could help him. He took out his phone and dialled his mentor, the bearded professor.

The professor was clear. 'You have no choice, Harry. You have to confront him and ask him to leave. *Immediately*. Look, I'm a little busy right now, and we can discuss this in detail in the evening. But the situation is clear. Just sack him right away.'

And that's exactly what Harry did. He summoned Imaan to his room and placed the bill in front of him. Being the smart guy that he was, Imaan tried to put the blame on the supplier. But this approach fizzled out when Harry told him he had already spoken to the supplier. Completely cornered by now, Imaan was quiet. But Harry was not. 'Imaan, I want your resignation letter right now. With immediate effect!' Left with no choice, Imaan had to agree. He resigned and was relieved of his duties on the spot.

That evening, Harry simply had to meet his mentor. And the professor did not disappoint him. For a change, they met at a coffee shop. 'Too much beer—I'm gaining weight,' said the professor.

'Sir, there is one thing I have not been able to understand,' said Harry. 'In one of your webinars, you were talking about inflated auto and taxi bills. And you had said, "Your purpose is not to find fault with your employee, or to tell him he is a crook. Your objective is to let him know that you are aware of the inflated bills. And he will get the message." But this time you clearly and unequivocally asked me to sack the guy. I did what you suggested, but I'm a bit confused. Why this difference in approach?'

As usual, the professor smiled and stroked his beard. 'Young man, when dealing with people, there is no black and white. There are shades of grey. What both these guys were doing was wrong. But you see, inflating auto claims is a very common practice. You do not need to submit any attached proof, and therefore a lot of people do it. I would go so far as to say that many people think it's their birthright.

'Is this right? Is it ethical? Of course not. But is it changeable? In many cases, yes. And if you sack all these people, you'll need to sack half your office. Therefore, it's better to try and get the guy to realize that it's been noticed. Hopefully, that'll get him to change. Of course, if he still doesn't, well, use the chopper. In the other case, however, it was a clear criminal offence. It was a fraud. And such people have to be shown the door. No option.'

And that was that. The two of them drained their respective cups and walked out into the cold Delhi night. Leaving Harry with one simple thought, 'How right the professor was. Managing people is a grey area. It cannot be black and white!'

So that was our friend, Harry. A true DREAM Founder, who led from the front, respected people, developed them, believed in communication, and treated them like his family. And much, much more.

But at the same time, he did not take any nonsense from them!

And that's the story of Harry.

Let's Meet Deepinder Goyal, founder and CEO, Zomato

What do you think of when you hear the name Zomato? Yummy kababs? Mouth-watering tandoori chicken? Or, for vegetarians, delicious idlis, dripping with sambhar and coconut chutney? Right? But have you ever met the brain behind Zomato—the guy who started it all? No? Well, here's your chance. Meet Deepinder Goyal, the founder and CEO of the phenomenally successful Zomato. The person who has made the brand a household name all over the country. My junior from IIT Delhi, who actually stayed in the same room in Aravali hostel as I did. When I requested Deepinder to share his experiences for the benefit of the readers of this book, he was more than willing (after all, you can't say no to your senior from college, can you 😊?). And this is what he had to say:

> The most important characteristic of a DREAM Founder is adaptability. Everything else is a given—he must have a dream, he must be passionate as well as knowledgeable about the business, he must be great at execution, etc., etc. Those are obvious. But what really sets him apart from the rest, is flexibility. His willingness and ability to adapt to what is happening around him. Don't for a moment imagine that things will remain what they are today. The business environment will change, technology will change, the needs of the market will change, government regulations will change. And as a founder, you have no choice. You cannot have fixed ideas. You need to adapt to these changes if you want to be truly successful. You must be willing to challenge your beliefs.
>
> Remember, your ego should not come in the way. If you've taken a decision and you need to accept the fact that it's not working, well, do it. Change your decision. I have seen too many

founders who are stuck in decisions they have taken in the past, and are unwilling to accept the fact that they need to adapt.

Let me share my own personal experience. When we started Zomato, it was a website where restaurants could list themselves, and customers would review them. That's it. There was no food delivery. In fact, in the year 2011, my co-founder put out a post saying that we would not be getting into the food delivery business. And look where we are today. Our primary business is food delivery. That's what I mean by adaptability!

Incidentally, what applies to founders applies to the rest of the team as well. Don't add on people who are stuck in their thinking. Try and recruit those who are able and willing to change—without their egos getting in the way. And once you've got them, your responsibility as a founder is to support them. Give them opportunities. Nurture them. Let them develop. Give them a chance to grow—even though they will make mistakes in the process.

Finally, let me leave you with one thought. You can listen to lots of people—and many of them will give you good advice. But as a founder, it is you who needs to take a call. It's your company, and it's your decision, not theirs!

And with that, my best wishes to all budding DREAM Founders reading this book.

Thanks a lot, Deepinder. It was great meeting you. And your advice will definitely help our young and perhaps not-so-young founders.

Section III

Execution, Execution, Execution

13

The PERSISTENT Business:
iDream Once Again

By now, I'm sure you understand the term DREAM Founder. And I hope you are well on your way to becoming one. But at this stage, I have a question for you. What about the business itself? Just as we have DREAM Founders, don't we have DREAM Businesses as well?

Actually, we do. And we call these PERSISTENT businesses. An acronym that I had coined along with my close friend and co-author, Sushanto Mitra, in an earlier book, *Funding Your Start-Up: And Other Nightmares*. Which, by the way, has also been published by Penguin Random House India. You might want to pick up a copy of that book as well. Don't worry—I'm happy to treat you to coffee and pastries whenever we meet, which will more than cover the cost of the book 😊. And, of course, sign both books.

But just in case you want to save that miserable amount of money, I've included a summary of the PERSISTENT model here.

You see, a PERSISTENT business follows a few simple guidelines. Which are:

- P: PROBLEM. Are you solving a problem for the customer?
- E: EARNINGS MODEL. How will you make money?
- R: RISKS and how you will mitigate them
- S: SIZE of the MARKET
- I: INNOVATION
- S: SCALABILITY
- T: TEAM, starting with the founders
- E: ENTRY BARRIERS
- N: NICHE. Where the market is crowded, identify a large enough, non-crowded niche
- T: TRACTION

Interestingly, in our experience of mentoring lots of start-ups, we have realized that successful start-ups tend to follow this PERSISTENT framework, whereas failures usually miss out on one or more parameters, such as size of the market, team, risks or, in fact, any of the others. And that gives founders as well as potential founders a great way to figure out whether or not they are likely to be successful. Mind you, there is no guarantee for success—even god cannot guarantee that. But I'm sure you would want to improve your chances, wouldn't you?

Anyhow, to understand what a PERSISTENT business is, let's go back to our wonderful start-up, iDream. We start with the 'P' in PERSISTENT, which stands for PROBLEM. You must solve a problem for the customer—otherwise you don't have a business! And iDream was clearly solving a massive problem—that of providing quality education in government schools.

And then, of course, the big issue: The customer has to pay you for solving his problem—and that's the EARNINGS MODEL, or the 'E' in PERSISTENT. Or at least *someone* has to pay you. For instance, in the case of iDream, the payment did not come from the school but from large organizations through their CSR funds. And later on, from state governments. Just remember, if you do not get payment, you are not running a business.

Anyhow, to get back to our earnings model, it is based on two things—revenues and profits. Revenues should be clear—that's what the customer pays you. But what about profits?

Aha, that's a tricky one. And we'll start by understanding the concept of unit economics.

Unit Economics

The term unit economics simply means earnings or profitability at the level of each unit. What is a unit, you might ask? It's actually one transaction. In the case of iDream, installing one TabLab in a school—with an average of twenty tablets—is one transaction, and therefore one unit.

Now here's an important definition:

> The revenue earned from this transaction, minus the direct cost of executing the transaction, gives you the earnings at the unit level.

I hope this is clear. If not, please read this definition again and again till it is. In the case of iDream, the revenue was clear—it came from the CSR funds it received for this one TabLab. And, of course, the costs would include the costs of buying the tablets as well as the visits to support the installation of the TabLab. But— and this is very important—*it would not include overheads such as office rent and salaries*. These were overheads that were required for the entire operation, and not just for one TabLab. Fortunately, the CSR funds iDream got for each TabLab were higher than the direct expenses for implementing that TabLab. And therefore, this business was profitable at the level of the unit. In other words, it had positive unit economics. And this is key—at the very least, any business needs to have positive earnings at the level of the unit. If not, the more transactions you have—in this case, the more TabLabs you set up—the more you lose.

Now, I'm sure you have two questions. Perhaps more than two, but I'll just answer two over here. Does the unit economics of your business have to be positive from day one? Actually, no! Sometimes, you might want to start by offering your product or service at a discount, simply to get your first few customers. Over time, once your services become popular and customers are hooked, well, you can happily charge more. Which means—and this is important—in the early days of your business, the unit economics could be negative. But that's acceptable as long as there is a plan to ultimately make it positive.

And now for the second question. Is positive unit economics sufficient to ensure overall profitability in your business? At the level of the company? Of course not! Remember, unit economics only covers the direct cost of selling a unit. It does not cover the overheads of the business such as rentals, marketing, salaries, etc.

Okay, I can see that this is becoming complex financial jugglery, and I can already notice your head drooping, so let me take some figures. By the way, these are fictitious figures—I can't reveal the real ones, you see? Let's assume that the direct cost of setting up a twenty-tablet TabLab is Rs 5 lakh. And let's also assume that they charge the sponsor Rs 8 lakh to set it up. That means that the unit economics of the business is positive, because they make a profit of Rs 3 lakh for every TabLab they set up. Now, let's further assume that they set up ten TabLabs in a month. Clearly, they make a profit of Rs 30 lakh per month.

But we have only considered direct costs so far. We haven't counted overheads such as rentals, salaries and marketing. Let's assume those overheads are Rs 36 lakh per month. This means that at the level of the company or business, they are actually making a loss of (36—30) or Rs 6 lakh per month.

You see? To be profitable at the level of the company, positive unit economics is just one of the conditions you need to satisfy.

You must also sell a sufficient number of units, so that the overheads are taken care of. In our case, to cover the overheads of the business, iDream would need to install twelve TabLabs per month. This would give it a direct profit of (12 x 3) or Rs 36 lakh per month. And that would neutralize the overheads, so the company would break even. It would become profitable only if the volumes were higher than this.

And now you can breathe easy, because that's the end of this complex financial discourse.

The Rest of the PERSISTENT Framework

Now to get back to our PERSISTENT model. The next letter in the model is 'S', which stands for SIZE of the MARKET. Critical, isn't it? Because if you have a small market, you will stop growing at some stage. And I'm sure you don't want to build a start-up that grows up to, say, Rs 50 lakh and then quietly says, 'Enough. Can't grow any more. I will now stagnate!' So, size is critical. But sometimes, even large markets can be hugely crowded, with lots of competitors. Possibly even huge ones. Take the case of iDream. There are so many companies out there in the edtech space. Starting with that giant, Byju's. So how would the founders of iDream get into this rat race and compete?

Aha. That's exactly the point. They didn't. They identified a subset within this education space that was not crowded. Something that we call a NICHE—the 'N' in our PERSISTENT model, which itself was large enough. Namely, the affordable education space in both English as well as regional languages. A huge space, wasn't it? And not crowded. Which is why our young founders are thriving and growing! So that's the message. The size of the market is critical, but if it is crowded, identify a large enough, non-crowded niche within it!

Then, of course, we have the next 'S' in our model, namely SCALABILITY. In very simple terms, the ability to grow fast.

Obviously, this is critical to your business. Because if you don't grow rapidly, your competitor will (and in any case, it always feels as though she is growing faster than you, doesn't it?). She will eat into your market share, take away your customers, and potentially kill you. Which is why scalability is so critical.

And that brings me to one of the most common questions I have been asked. Namely, 'Is my start-up scalable? And if it is not, how do I make it scalable?' To answer this question, I'll compare three different online tutorial classes. The first one is run by a brilliant tutor called Nath Sir (not related to me), who is very popular with both kids and parents. The second one is an online learning platform called Singh Sir's classes, started by Singh Sir, who is as popular as Nath Sir. But the fundamental difference between the two is that in Singh Sir's classes there is no live teaching. Yes, Singh Sir does appear and takes sessions, but it's all pre-recorded. Of course, there is a lot of animation and the sessions are highly interactive. But—and I must repeat this—there is no live interaction between teacher and students.

Question: Which of these is a more scalable business? Actually, the answer should be obvious, isn't it? Kids come to Nath Sir because of Nath Sir. And obviously this gentleman has limited time—twenty-four hours a day, in case you didn't know. During the mornings, children are at school, so no classes are possible till around 4 p.m. And of course, the poor guy needs to sleep—so let's assume he stops his classes at 10 p.m. That gives him six hours a day. That's it. He cannot scale his business further. But what if he engages other tutors? Remember, I told you that kids come here and, of course, parents are willing to shell out their hard-earned black money—because of Nath Sir. Not Pathak Sir, or Ghosh Sir or Venkat Sir. No sir. It has to be Nath Sir. So, there you have it. This business cannot be scaled up, because kids would not come for Pathak Sir's classes, or Ghosh Sir's classes, or . . .

And what about Singh Sir's classes? Well, you have no live human interaction—only recorded sessions by Singh Sir. And once this gentleman has recorded all his sessions, he just sits back and relaxes. Because you can have thousands of students attending his recorded classes every day. There's no limit, is there? So, which of these business models is more scalable? Obviously, Singh Sir's classes! Because it's all technology. No human involvement.

And now, let's look at the third online classes started by Gupta Sir. Gupta Sir had read both my books (thank you, Gupta Sir). And therefore, he knew how to make his business scalable. But he didn't want to go the 'Singh Sir' route. He believed that it was important to have some live sessions as well. So, he provided everything that Singh Sir did, but in addition, he had a team of teachers who would take live sessions to clear doubts.

How scalable was this model? Well, definitely more scalable than Nath Sir's classes. Because the business was not limited by Nath Sir's availability and could grow big. But not as scalable as Singh Sir's classes. Because to grow, the business needed to add teachers. Not just teachers—great teachers. Otherwise, the business would simply collapse. And finding great teachers takes time, thereby slowing down growth. So, Gupta Sir's classes were somewhere between Nath Sir's classes and Singh Sir's classes in scalability.

To take another example, let's look at two highly successful software companies—Microsoft and Infosys. Which of them is more scalable? Microsoft, isn't it? Because Infosys is a people-dependent business. If they wanted to increase their revenues significantly, they would have to add a proportionate number of programmers and analysts. And then train them. And that also means they would need to add computers for all these people, new buildings to house them, and of course, infrastructure within these buildings. But all this is not easy to do in a hurry. On the other hand, Microsoft is a product-oriented business with products such as Windows and MS-Office. If they wanted to increase revenues, they would certainly not add proportionate manpower. All they would need to do is to spend more on marketing, and perhaps add some sales guys.

I hope you get the message. Businesses that are dependent on adding proportionate manpower and infrastructure to grow, are not the most scalable. Whereas those which are product-based or purely digital, are.

Incidentally, nowhere am I saying that Infosys is not a great business. Of course it is. And it has grown tremendously over the years. All I am saying is, its growth is dependent on a proportionate increase in manpower and infrastructure, and therefore, the rate at which it can grow is limited, compared to a pure digital or product business. Happy?

So now, let's get back to our very own start-up, iDream. A pure product-oriented business and that too, digital. No proportionate increase in manpower needed for growth. And therefore? You've guessed it—it's a highly scalable business. QED.

And now for the risks in the business—the 'R' in the PERSISTENT model. No business is risk-free. And one of the biggest risks to your business is the possibility of competition coming in, taking away your market share and potentially killing you. For which you need what we call an ENTRY BARRIER—the 'E' in PERSISTENT. Sometimes called competitive advantage, or even moat. What's an entry barrier? Very simply, a barrier that you have built, which prevents your competitor from entering your business, and potentially beating the hell out of you. Incidentally, if you have an INNOVATIVE solution (the 'I' in the PERSISTENT model), possibly with a patent or two, that makes a great entry barrier.

Now, let's take a look at iDream once again. Did it have an entry barrier? Of course, it did! The founders had developed a huge amount of educational content in both Hindi and English, along with a powerful Learning Management System (LMS). And they had also bought out content in many of the other Indian languages. If a competitor were to enter their business, they would first need to develop an LMS, and create the content—or perhaps buy out parts of it. And that would take time, wouldn't it?

So, that was a very neat entry barrier that iDream had built into the business.

Now, if you've been listening to me—and I hope you have—you would have noticed something interesting. True, iDream had built an entry barrier because of all its content as well as the LMS. And it would take several months for competition to catch up. But what would the founders do in the meantime? Would they sit back, rest on their laurels, and watch Netflix? Safe in the knowledge that they were now unbeatable?

Of course not. Remember, their competition would take a few months to build all the content and software to compete with them. After that, what? No entry barrier any more! And therefore, it was important for our friends to continuously increase the entry barrier in their business, so that a competitor could never catch up. And that's a vital message for you, dear founder. Entry barriers are not permanent. Since competition would always try and catch up, you need to keep enhancing them month on month, year on year. So even if your competitor does try and catch up, it is chasing a shifting target.

And finally, the last two pieces in the PERSISTENT model. The first 'T' stands for TEAM. Starting with the founders. We have a saying in the world of start-ups, 'If you have a great business model but an average team, the business is likely to fail.' Conversely, 'If the business model is average but the team is great, well, the team will figure out a way to make the model work.' And the team, of course, starts with the founders. Who need to be—you've guessed it—DREAM Founders. Like Puneet and Rohit.

Finally, you may have a great business model, highly scalable, with a terrific entry barrier and a solid earnings model. In short, you might satisfy all the nine components of the PERSISTENT model that we've seen so far. But what's the final proof? The final proof, my friend, is the TRACTION in the business! Are you getting customers? Are they increasing, month on month? Are existing customers staying on, or are they quitting? Are they paying? Are your revenues increasing month on month? You see? —Traction. Real customers and real revenues.

And did our friends at iDream get traction? Of course, they did! When I started spending time with them, they had implemented their solution in thirty schools. And within just a few years, at the time of writing this book, they had reached several thousand government schools with their affordable learning solution. Now if that isn't traction, I don't know what is!

Finally, here's a table that summarizes the PERSISTENT business model of iDream:

		iDream
P	Problem: Are you solving a real problem?	Definitely, given the poor quality of education in many government schools.
E	Earnings Model	Revenues through CSR funds as well as state governments. Unit economics positive.
R	Risks, and how you will mitigate them.	No major risk.
S	Size of the market	Massive.
I	Innovation	Vernacular content. Unique concept of TabLab.
S	Scalability	High, given the fact that it is a product business, with low manual involvement.
T	Team, starting with the founders.	DREAM Founders.
E	Entry Barriers	Learning Management System, as well as the large amount of content they had. Building the brand over time.
N	Niche: When the market is crowded, identify a niche.	Government and other affordable schools.
T	Traction	Presence in several thousand schools across the country, at the time of writing this book.

DREAM Founder or PERSISTENT Business—Which One Should I Follow?

And now, I can see you itching to raise an issue. And I must congratulate you, because most founders I have spoken to, have raised the same issue. You see, I've given you two wonderful frameworks—A DREAM Founder, and a PERSISTENT business model (at least, they seem wonderful to me). But isn't there an overlap between these two?

My friend, you are dead right. Of course, there is. But isn't that completely natural? After all, it's the founder who creates and runs the business, so there is bound to be an overlap between the two. As an example, a DREAM Founder needs to dream big. But that's only possible if the size of the market is large, isn't it? As another example, a PERSISTENT business needs a great team. Which starts with the DREAM Founder himself. Or take a look at the entry barrier in PERSISTENT businesses. One possible way to develop an entry barrier is to build your brand, which means marketing, of course. Which in turn is part of execution. And you would ideally like an innovative solution, which is part of building your product. Once again, a part of execution.

As you can see, there will be a lot of overlap. But there will also be areas that are unique to one or the other. Personally, I have found it useful to use both. And where there is an overlap, well frankly, it doesn't matter a damn which one you use (apologies for the term—and I hope the editor doesn't delete it, because I consider it very, very expressive). Use whatever you are comfortable with.

Unless, of course, you are planning to do a PhD on the subject!

14

What They Don't Tell You about Marketing: The Message

And now to continue with the BOMB approach. I will not spend much time on the expansion of the first two letters of the acronym, namely 'B'—BUILD your PRODUCT, and 'O'—OPERATIONS, because these are very specific to each business. Instead, I will discuss these when I take up individual cases. If you're not okay with that, too bad!

However, what I *will* spend time on is one of the most critical pieces in the puzzle, namely 'M' for MARKETING. Which will get you those elusive customers. Who bring along that black briefcase (sometimes it's also brown), containing those wonderful, crisp rupee notes. Which you can count over and over with a smirk—behind closed doors, of course. Or if you want to be boring, you might get the money transferred online into your bank account.

Now, I must clarify something here. Yes, I must. You have probably started reading this chapter thinking that it will give you a full-fledged MBA in marketing. Or, at the very least, it will cover *Marketing Management* by Philip Kotler, the guru of marketing. I was right, wasn't I? You did expect this? My friend, let me get a few facts straight. I am not attempting to replace Philip Kotler. If I did, this book would probably be eight hundred pages thick and would cost over a thousand rupees. Which you, as a self-respecting founder on the edge of penury, would never be able to afford.

No sir, I wanted you to read this book. I wanted it to be affordable. So did Radhika, my editor at Penguin Random House India. And therefore, we decided, in our wisdom, to restrict the contents.

How? Well, I've already told you that I have spent lots of time with young founders (older ones too, but I prefer the young ones—more enthusiastic and bubbly, you see). I looked at the questions they were asking. And the blunders some of them were making. Interestingly, I found that most of the issues were common, and so were the solutions. And that's where I made my decision. I would focus on the common issues that all these founders were facing and try and give you solutions to them. Hopefully, that will take care of all your questions. Incidentally, many of the issues I'll discuss might not even be available in Mr Kotler's book. So, you can actually buy both, although Mr Kotler probably doesn't realize that I'm promoting his book 😊.

Also, this will not be a thousand-page treatise on how to market on Facebook or Instagram, or any other social media platform that might suddenly explode in the future. Similarly, I will not be telling you how to get backlinks to ensure search engine optimization. Or how to optimize your marketing campaign on Amazon. There is a good reason for this. You see, the digital environment is changing by the day. Every now and then, you have a new entrant in the crowded social media space. First it was Facebook, and then Instagram and Twitter. And now you have Koo in India. And suddenly Clubhouse has sprung up from nowhere. God knows what else will come up by the time you read this book.

To complicate matters further, all these guys change their policies on a regular basis. So, a campaign that might be optimal today may not be so great a year later. And what would you do if you've bought my book and Facebook suddenly changes its policy? Would you call me up desperately and ask me to revise whatever I have written because it's out of date? And then will you buy the next edition? And the next? Of course not. Therefore, I decided to talk about general principles, along with some examples, because these principles will remain. And I know you are intelligent—so use that intelligence to apply these principles to whatever exists.

One more comment—and a very critical one. Please remember, no amount of marketing can replace your product. If you have a poor product, or a product that the customer doesn't want, well, you cannot cover it up through phenomenal marketing. No sir, the product and marketing go hand in hand!

Now, before I start with my lecture (please remember, I have been a professor for twenty years), I will divide the entire subject of marketing into two parts (I'm sure there are wise men out there who will be able to divide it into four or seven or perhaps even twenty-three parts, but I'll stick to my two parts, thank you very much). And I'll call these two parts the 'Message', and the 'Medium'. What do these mean? Very simple—the message is what you are saying to the potential buyer, and the medium refers to how you reach him or her—whether through huge advertisements in newspapers, or social media, or emails, or good old face-to-face sales calls. In my forty-odd years of experience, I have found it extremely important to look at marketing through these two lenses, and that's exactly what I'll be doing in this book.

Clear? So, let's start with the message. I'll cover the medium in the next chapter.

The Concept of WYKM

Let me take you to a south Indian restaurant (by the way, I have taken a south Indian restaurant purely as an example. The same thing would apply to a Bengali restaurant, or an Oriya restaurant, or a Punjabi dhaba, or . . .). Anyway, once you are seated, you ask the waiter, '*Kya hai khaane ko* (What's on the menu)?' And the waiter rattles off at a speed of around a hundred miles per hour, 'Rice idli, rava idli, podi idli, fried idli, onion uthappam, tomato uthappam, vegetable uthappam, paneer uthappam, plain dosa, masala dosa, paper dosa, vada sambhar . . .'

But, of course, you haven't got anything out of his rapid-fire speech, so you ask him to repeat the menu, but slower. And he slows down his spiel by perhaps a few inches per hour, and starts off again, 'Rice idli, rava idli, podi idli, fried idli, onion uthappam, tomato uthappam, vegetable uthappam, paneer uthappam . . .'

By which time you've lost patience and you still haven't figured out what the menu is, so you simply ask for idli sambhar, because that's the one thing they are likely to have anyway!

Sounds familiar? Of course, it does. So, what's the problem?

Obvious, isn't it? The waiter is trying to tell you too, too much. Consequently, you get nothing out of it. And that, by the way, is true of any form of communication. Too much being said. Remember, communication is not just what the communicator wants to say. Communication is what the recipient receives and ultimately absorbs and remembers. And human beings cannot be expected to listen to multiple issues, absorb them, and remember them.

Makes sense? So, let's take a few examples:

- Maggi two-minute noodles
- *Achhe din aane waale hain* (Prime Minister Narendra Modi in his 2014 campaign)
- Yes, we can (Barack Obama)

Now since you are smart, I'm sure you can figure out how these three messages are different from what our poor young waiter was trying to communicate.

That's right. Each of these messages communicates one simple idea. Take a minute and read the three messages again. See what I mean? One simple, key idea, which is easy to understand, absorb, and therefore remember. Nothing huge, not hundreds of words, or tens of ideas. One simple message—that's it. And therefore, ladies and gentlemen, the recipient gets the message and remembers it!

We have a term for this very important concept in communication. We call it WYKM, which is short for 'What's Your Key Message?' This concept is critical to any good communication, and therefore to your marketing message as well. For your customer to get and absorb what you are saying, your message must be short and crisp. Ideally one single idea or at best, two or three. Definitely not five or ten. Accepted? So, let's get back to marketing.

What should your key message be?

Aha, for that, I'll first need to introduce you to another concept. The concept of pain.

The Painful Way to Market

I have a favourite story that I must tell you. Many, many years ago, perhaps before you were born, the first 'made in India' microwave oven was launched. And I still remember their advertisement—a half page ad splashed across dailies such as the *Times of India* and the *Hindustan Times*. Obviously, it had a photograph of the oven. I don't remember the exact wording of the ad, but it went something like this:

> You loved the way she walked
> You loved the way she smiled
> You loved the way she spoke
> So, you married her . . .
>   . . . and put her into the kitchen!

Now, I would like you to shut this book for a few minutes and think. Fold the page as a bookmark, if you wish. Think, think. Who is this ad aimed at?

Husbands, naturally.

And if any husband were to read this ad, what do you think his reaction would be?

Extreme guilt, isn't it? In fact, when this ad appeared, I was married and so were many of my male colleagues. Believe me, we were all extremely embarrassed to see this ad. All of us wanted to hide in the nearest corner we could find. Our immediate reaction was, 'My god, this is exactly what I have done. How could I be so unfair?'

Now, if you've understood what happened, you have understood a fundamental principle of marketing (of course, if you haven't understood, you are probably unmarried and carefree, but believe me, at some stage you *will* understand). Anyhow, for the unmarried reader, let me explain. Remember the first letter in our PERSISTENT framework—'P' for problem? Where I had said that you must solve a problem for your customer, otherwise he will not buy your product? And this is the crucial bit—the customer must feel the pain that the problem is causing. The more the pain, the bigger the perception of the problem, and therefore the higher the likelihood of the customer buying the product. In the case of the microwave oven, the pain was in the form of guilt. So, the manufacturer maximized guilt in the mind of the husband, and increased the chances of him buying the oven.

And, by the way, this was just one simple, hard-hitting idea. In other words, it was—the WYKM, of course!

And that brings me to the crux of what I've been trying to say. Read this carefully and absorb it:

'To maximize the chances of your customer buying your product or service, maximize the pain. Of course, your product or service must be a solution to that pain.'

Incidentally, the corollary is equally important, 'Don't create so much pain that he commits suicide 😊!'

By the way, I must tell you what happened in my case. The ad had created so much guilt in my mind that I was all set to buy this microwave oven. And to hell with the cost! Fortunately, my wife Rajni was abroad visiting her brother at that time, and when she came home, she brought with her a shining new imported microwave oven!

Just look around you, and you will see this principle in action in many ads—whether on TV, on the Internet, on the radio or just about anywhere else. For instance, when you walk into the office of a travel agent (yes, some people still prefer that over making an online booking), what do you see just behind the receptionist? A huge poster of the snowy mountains of Switzerland, isn't it? And you've just walked in from the 43-degree summer in the month of May in Delhi. Desperately wiping off your sweat. At that moment, what do you feel, my friend? You are in the sweltering heat of Delhi, but you could easily be in the snows of Switzerland. Pain, isn't it? And therefore, your likelihood of buying a package tour to Switzerland goes up!

Or take the example of TV ads for health insurance. You are lying down peacefully in your bed, when suddenly the bed gets converted into a hospital bed, and your bedroom into a hospital room. Painful? Yes, because health insurance is what the advertiser is trying to sell you. Or ads for toothpaste which show a person grimacing at the pain in his or her tooth. Or ads for a deodorant which show a girl looking disgusted because her admirer and (hopeful) boyfriend has bad body odour. Or . . .

In fact, let's try and apply this approach to a couple of start-ups that we have met in this book. Starting with Instamojo. Remember, in this case, the customer is a small business that wants to go online.

What about a message like this:

'The world is going online.
Are you missing out on customers because you are not?
Now you don't need to.
Because now you have Instamojo!'

Works, doesn't it? One simple WYKM, which creates pain—and Instamojo has a solution which relieves that pain.

And now for the other one—Trainerbhai. Remember, the company was into sales training for businesses. And with very strong follow-up through its online portal. Let's try out this message:

'Have your sales training programmes been a waste of time and money? Because your salespeople have forgotten what they have learnt, and gone back to what they were doing earlier?

Presenting Trainerbhai. We believe in follow-up. So your salespeople do not forget!'

You see? It's actually very easy. All you need to do is to create a simple WYKM that creates pain in the mind of the customer. In the first case, it was the pain of missing out on online customers. And in the second one, the pain of a wasted sales training programme. Of course, you may also have the mandatory good-looking model smiling seductively at you, even if it is for a product like a toilet cleaner. But I'm sure you don't need to read my book to learn this. In any case, I am definitely not the right person to teach you these tricks.

So as a founder, you need to figure out what your WYKM is. And having created this, you are all set for the next step. Where you need to reach this message to the customer.

But how? Do you advertise on social media? Do you put up massive hoardings? Do you make presentations in college campuses? Yes, dear reader, these are the questions you need to ask now. Namely, what is the medium you will use?

But not today. I notice you're looking a bit tired. Do take a break. Come back tomorrow and turn the page. And we'll take a look at the second issue in marketing—the medium.

15

What They Don't Tell You about Marketing: The Medium

The Basic Question: Sales Versus Marketing?

Let's start with an old question. What's the difference between sales and marketing? My friend, if you were to ask twenty different people, you will probably get twenty different answers. So let me try and simplify it for you by taking some examples. Meeting the purchase manager of a corporation and convincing him to buy your product, is sales. Running a campaign on Facebook or Instagram, is marketing. Convincing a customer who has walked into your retail shop that sells mobile phones, is sales. Advertising in the newspapers or on hoardings, is marketing. As you can see, sales is generally one-to-one, typically with a human interface, whereas marketing is one-to-many, and usually does not involve a human interface. But things are not always so simple. When someone from a call centre calls you up in the middle of your peaceful Sunday afternoon nap, what would you call it? It's one-to-one, so it should be sales, shouldn't it? Actually telesales. But just to confuse you, some people call it telemarketing. And that's why I had said right in the beginning, there are no standard definitions for these two terms. However, one common school of thought is what I've mentioned earlier. In other words, sales is one-to-one and usually involves a human interface, whereas marketing is one-to-many. And that's the definition I will use in this book.

By the way, this definition makes it fairly easy to figure out what to use where. Let's take a few examples. If your client is the government of India, or perhaps state governments, there is no point in advertising on Facebook. Instead, you would need to identify the person or persons in the government who might be interested, fix an appointment with him or her and make a presentation. That's one-to-one, and therefore sales.

Another example: If you are in the business of providing software solutions for HR (human resources), your customers would be HR executives in companies. Here you have two possible situations. There are perhaps some companies where you are already in touch with the HR executive, so you can fix up an appointment and sell to her—and that's sales again. Incidentally, that's a huge benefit of getting investors to fund your start-up, since they help you with contacts. On the other hand, there would be hundreds, perhaps thousands of organizations where you do not have any contacts. You could then get hold of the email IDs of the HR executives—perhaps through their website or even through LinkedIn, and send mailers to all of them. That's marketing. A few of these people might respond. Fix up an appointment with these people and meet them. And those are sales calls. In this example therefore, you started with marketing and ended up making sales calls.

On the other hand, if you are in a B2C (business-to-customer) business such as Myntra or Bigbasket, your audience is completely scattered. You simply don't know who your potential customers are. And therefore, you would probably run a campaign on Facebook or Instagram. Or if you have the money, you might run full-page ads in newspapers. Which is one-to-many, with no human being involved, and therefore we would call it marketing.

You must also remember that high-value products or services—such as cars or homes—usually need a significant sales effort. Can you imagine a buyer clicking on a Facebook ad for a car and then casually clicking 'Buy Now' and paying perhaps 20 lakh on the spot? No, of course not. He would need to visit the car showroom, check out all the features, perhaps do a test drive. Maybe bash up the car just a couple of times to see how it ties in with his driving skills, or lack of them. And only then would the buyer go ahead and purchase the car (a new piece, naturally. Not the one that just got bashed up). On the other hand, if you were selling, say, healthy biscuits online (if there is such a thing), you only need marketing. You simply put up your product on your e-commerce site, or perhaps on Amazon or Flipkart. And then you place ads—perhaps on Facebook. And hopefully, enough people click and buy the biscuits. No one-to-one sales required.

Finally, on the subject of sales I have one question for you. Perhaps the most important question of all: Who is the chief salesperson in your company?

Ha, ha, it's obvious, isn't it? *You*, dear founder. You have to show the way. No sitting in an ivory tower, setting targets and shouting at young people who don't meet them. No sir, you have to lead sales. You have to be the chief person who brings in the business, and who the others look up to!

What did you say? You can't sell? Well then, please learn. Start selling. Make mistakes. That's the only way to learn. And please don't tell me it's not your job. *It is your job.* Remember the PERFECT ATTITUDE in chapter 4?

Fixed Versus Variable Cost Marketing

And now for a very common question that founders have asked me, 'Sir, to grow my business I need to spend money on marketing. Now, I don't have money, so I need funding. But till I show growth, investors are not willing to fund me. So, what should I do?'

Familiar question? Of course it is. Founders of early-stage start-ups will always face this problem. No money, therefore no marketing spend, therefore no growth, therefore no money. It's a chicken and egg situation—without chickens, you can't get eggs, and without eggs, you can't get chickens. So, what do you do?

Fortunately, there are ways around this problem—at least to some extent. So please read on. Let me tell you the story of three similar start-ups called NoSkills, PoorSkills, and LousySkills, operating in three different cities, namely Mumbai, Bangalore and Delhi. All three companies were offering online courses that would help college students build their skills, in fields such as computer programming and digital marketing. And in the process, get them more 'job-ready'. All three had built great products, complete with 'educational' videos of good-looking young models, who they called faculty. You see, all the founders realized that to build skills, it was important to get students glued to their laptop screens. And what better way than to have good-looking teachers?

Anyhow, our focus here is not on the looks of these teachers. It's on marketing, so let's not digress. Like most wonderful start-ups out there, none of them had any significant funds to spend on marketing. So, what did they do? Well, let's take NoSkills first. The founders of NoSkills realized that their target segment was college students. So, they decided to put up hoardings near a few college campuses. They believed that college students would see these ads, get interested and sign up for their skill-building courses. Which made sense. As a result, they did get some inquiries from students. And some of these students did join them. The only problem was that these hoardings were expensive, and the founders ran out of money very fast.

Now for PoorSkills. The founders here were more tech-savvy. They had heard a lot about social media marketing. They decided, in their wisdom, to place ads on Facebook. The ads would be seen by lots of students, but only those who were interested would click on them. And that's when PoorSkills would pay for the ad. In other words, *PoorSkills would pay for the ad only when a student was interested and therefore clicked on it.* Once again, these guys were able to get some students to register, but soon ran out of money.

And then of course, we had LousySkills. These founders didn't put up hoardings, and they didn't advertise on Facebook or Instagram. Instead, they appointed what are popularly known as campus ambassadors. Who? Actually, a few students in each college, whose job it was to locate interested students from their college and get them to register. Importantly, these ambassadors were paid a commission for each registration that they got. And this is critical, so I'll repeat it. *LousySkills paid their campus ambassadors only when a student registered and therefore paid up.* Of course, this start-up spent the least of all three and was able to get a few registrations, but there weren't too many. In fact, its growth was slower than that of NoSkills and PoorSkills.

So, where does that leave us? Which of these was the best approach? Ha ha, my friend. It's not so simple, so just pick up a cup of coffee—or rasam if you prefer—and read on.

Let me first define three stages in any kind of marketing that you might do. And we'll start with NoSkills. As I had mentioned, the founders had put up hoardings near college campuses. Many students would see these hoardings as they passed by (of course, if it were a lovey-dovey couple from campus, they would probably be gazing at each other, and the last thing they would want to look at is the stupid hoarding put up by NoSkills). Anyhow, let us assume that not everyone was fortunate enough to be part of such a couple, and therefore, at least these miserable students would see the hoarding. Now, the important issue is that these folks might or might not have been interested in the offering, but at least they would have seen it. And that's the first stage of marketing, which I'll call 'Awareness'. Incidentally, these are my terms. I'm not sure if Philip Kotler or any other marketing guru uses these terms, but that's irrelevant. If he doesn't agree with them, that's just too bad!

Anyhow, to get back to marketing, there would be some students who would glance at the hoarding—or curse it in case they banged into it—and then move on. Nothing further for them. But there would also be some who would be interested. 'Enhancing my skills? Good idea. Maybe it'll help me get a job'. Hopefully, there would be a few such people, and they would have moved on to the next stage, namely the 'Interest' stage, where they would at least be interested in exploring these courses further. What would these guys do? Well, NoSkills would have mentioned a phone number or an email ID on the hoarding and interested students would contact them.

After these interested students had spoken to someone at NoSkills, a few of them would realize that this was just the thing they had been waiting for since the age of two, so they would promptly register and pay their fee. In other words, these students would now have reached the third stage in the marketing process, the 'Purchase' stage.

So, these are the three stages in marketing—awareness, interest, and purchase.

And now for something extremely important. Of course, everything I've said in this book is extremely important, but so is this. NoSkills paid a fixed amount per month for each hoarding—whether people looked at it or not. Whether they were interested in it or not. Whether they ultimately registered and paid up or not. You see? NoSkills could have got a thousand people interested or just five, and they might have got a hundred registrations or zero, but they still paid a fixed amount per month, for the privilege of having their hoarding out there, irrespective of the result. And that, ladies and gentlemen, is called 'fixed cost marketing'.

Let's now take a look at PoorSkills, which had placed ads on Facebook and Instagram. Now, I don't want to write a full book on how Facebook works. Later perhaps. But you are aware that Facebook and other similar social media would be using some complex algorithms, which ensure that any ad is shown only to people who are likely to be interested. For instance, if you were part of a group which was into college education, well, Facebook was likely to show you the PoorSkills ad. And this is the key: Lots of people might see the ad, but only those who were interested would click on it, and thereby reach the website of PoorSkills. And Facebook would charge PoorSkills for each click. A thousand people or more might have seen the ad, and therefore been at the awareness stage. But PoorSkills would not pay for this. They would only pay for each person who clicked on the ad and therefore moved on to the interest stage.

Equally important, not everyone who clicked on the ad would register and pay up (the purchase stage). So, PoorSkills would pay for all those people who were interested, whether they finally bought the course or not.

And what about LousySkills? Well, the campus ambassador might get a bunch of students together and talk to them—the awareness stage. But LousySkills wouldn't pay for this. Some of these students might land up on the LousySkills website and check it out—the interest stage. Again, LousySkills wouldn't pay anything for this. No sir, LousySkills would pay their campus ambassador only when a student registered on their site and paid up. Which means that *they would spend on marketing only when they actually earned revenues*. Something that we call 'variable cost marketing'. Smart, wasn't it? No revenues, no marketing spend! By the way, in general, variable cost marketing requires you to appoint agents (let's call them sales partners), who get a commission for every sale made.

And just to complete the picture, the kind of marketing that PoorSkills did on Facebook is called 'semi-fixed cost marketing'. Where you spend only when the user is interested and therefore clicks on the link provided. But not when he or she buys! So, it is somewhere between fixed and variable cost marketing.

Let's take some more examples. TV ads, jingles on the radio, ads in newspapers and in cinema halls, etc., are all examples of fixed-cost marketing. Most digital advertising—including the well-known Google Ads—is semi-fixed cost, because you pay per click (so the person clicking is interested) but not per order (so the person might click but not buy). Influencer marketing, where you get a person who has a large number of followers on social media to talk about your product, is fixed cost marketing. Because you would pay the influencer per post on social media, whether or not people show interest. On the other hand, anything which is pure commission-based—such as appointing dealers or distributors, is variable cost marketing. So is referral-based marketing, where you get existing customers to get their friends to buy your product and get some sort of reward in return. Even a loyalty programme is variable cost marketing, because the customer gets his rewards only when he comes back and buys your product again and again.

Now, I hope things are clear so far. If not, please splash your face with cold water and read this section again. And again. Keep repeating this till you've got it!

Anyhow, assuming you've got it, here is some more gyan:

Question: Which of these is the best option?

Answer: It depends.

Question: On what?

Answer: Well, if you have no money, you really have no choice. It will have to be pure variable cost marketing. Where you spend only when your customer makes a purchase. In that sense, this is the most efficient form of marketing, because you pay only when the customer pays you. That's the positive side of variable cost marketing. The negative is that your reach is limited—unless, of course, your sales partner has a huge following—perhaps on social media. After all, how many people can he sell to?

What about semi-fixed cost marketing? In other words, ads on Facebook or Instagram? Well, here you are likely to get a far larger audience because lots of people would see your ad. You are not dependent on the limited reach of your sales partners any more. The flip side is that you need to spend for every person who clicks and therefore shows interest, whether he buys your product or not. This makes it a less efficient way of marketing than the pure variable cost variety.

Finally, what about fixed cost marketing? Well, this is likely to be the least efficient method, simply because you are paying for the hoarding, or for the ad to be displayed on TV, whether or not it generates interest. Whether or not the customer finally buys your product and pays you. In other words, you probably need to spend large amounts here. On the other hand, the awareness that it generates could be far higher than the other two kinds. After all, anyone walking down the road or watching TV can see the ad!

So, which one should you use? It really depends on what you are looking for. If you have no money, you have no choice—it will have to be variable cost marketing. If you have some money, it's a good idea to have a combination of variable and semi-fixed cost marketing. Hopefully, you'll build up revenues and therefore be able to sustain it. But if you are a late-stage start-up and want to do significant brand-building, fixed cost marketing is an interesting option to look at.

Of course, these are guidelines, not rules. No one will put you in jail if you want to do brand building purely through appointing distributors. But they are useful guidelines. Try them out.

Zero or Near-Zero Cost Marketing

Aha. No money at all? Well, fortunately, you do not need to commit suicide (in any case that's not a nice thing to do, so you shouldn't contemplate it anyway). There are ways to market your product without spending money at all. Not even when a sale is made. Something that we call zero cost marketing. So, let's look at some of the options.

First of all, there are some businesses which do not need massive newspaper ads or hoardings or Facebook marketing. Let's take a very simple example where you've set up an IT consulting company. Perhaps you and a couple of co-founders are the main consultants. And your clients are organizations—whether large or small. Now, you don't need a thousand clients to run your business successfully. All you need is perhaps three or four of them and you are in business.

Now tell me, do you really need to put up hoardings for these three or four clients? Do you need to advertise on Facebook? Of course not. How silly. Hopefully, you'll have a few contacts—and your investors could provide the rest. Hire a salesperson who meets these contacts. Or better still, meet them yourself—after all, you are the chief salesperson, aren't you? And maybe a few of them will try you out. That's it. No fancy, expensive campaigns. Just one-to-one sales. Where you will need to spend on one person's salary and perhaps some amount on travel. So, this is fixed cost marketing, but it is not likely to be too expensive. It's just one person's salary, after all. By the way, many B2B businesses just need one-to-one selling of the kind I've just described.

But hang on. I've spoken about getting three to four major clients. What if your business requires hundreds of them? Well, that's where you could use social media—Facebook, LinkedIn, Instagram and the like. By the way, I'm not talking about advertising here. I'm simply talking about putting up posts at zero cost. Where your contacts and friends can like the post or even comment on it. So, *their* contacts and friends see the post and so on. And someone down the chain who reads the post might actually be interested in buying your product. Social media presence is the primary method of marketing used by early-stage start-ups, simply because it does not involve any spend. Of course, you need to remember two things. First, you must build up lots of connections because that's how your message will spread far and wide. And second, your post must have interesting content. Content that others want to read. Otherwise, people will stop viewing it.

And then, of course, you could get press coverage. The press tends to write about interesting start-ups and innovative products, so you could be in business. Of course, if you are start-up number 147 doing more or less what the other 146 are doing, forget it. No magazine—whether online or physical—is going to write about you. The other issue is that you need to have contacts in the media, and that's where your investors can help.

Finally, there is another form of near-zero cost marketing that I need to talk about—something that I will call B2B2C marketing. Let's assume you had a start-up called ObeseFit, where you provided advice on fitness to individuals. This could be in the form of recorded videos, text, as well as live, personalized sessions. Now, you meet the HR head of Tata Consultancy Services (TCS). And since you are a crack salesperson, he is convinced—rightly so—that your offer would benefit his employees. So, what does he do? He sends an email to all his employees informing them about your service. And, of course, this email contains a link to ObeseFit. Those who are interested click on this link, and hopefully some of them register and pay up. And what have you spent? Absolutely nothing, except for the cost of the sales calls that you made to TCS, or Hindustan Unilever, or whichever company you've met. Brilliant, isn't it? An extremely popular approach, which we call B2B2C marketing. Because you first sell to the organization (the 'B'), which in turn helps you to sell to its employees (the 'Cs').

So, What Did iDream and Instamojo Do?

Now that you've understood the importance of choosing the right medium for your marketing campaign, let's go back to the two start-ups we have introduced so far. Starting with iDream. Initially, the founders needed to market the concept to corporate sponsors—those who would provide the CSR funds. These were basically a few large companies, and the founders simply looked for contacts where possible. Subsequently, they personally made one-to-one sales calls to the head of CSR. And so, it was effectively zero-cost marketing. Of course, they had travel expenses, but the overall marketing cost remained low. Later on, they started partnering with hardware vendors as well as system integrators, and made sales calls to state governments. In other words, they continued to use near-zero cost marketing.

But during and after Covid, when these guys started selling to individual students at home, they did it through partners such as smartphone dealers. Here, the partner would obviously take a commission for each tablet sold, but did not charge a fixed fee. In other words—yes, you've guessed it—this was variable cost marketing.

And what about Instamojo? They were also running a B2B business, but unlike iDream, their clients were not large corporates. Instead, as you would remember, they were small businesses such as ladies baking cakes at home, or tutors taking online classes, or even small travel agents. Now clearly, pure sales calls would not help Instamojo. For one thing, they had no idea who these small businesses were. In fact, many of them might simply be operating from home!

Therefore they had to do some level of advertising through social media, as well as on search engines such as Google, which fits into our category of semi-fixed cost marketing. They were also helped by the fact that their services went viral very fast. For instance, a customer of a lady who baked cakes might himself be running a small business. And if he was happy with the e-commerce solution as well as the payment mechanism provided, well, he himself could become an Instamojo customer. Which, if you're still awake, is zero-cost marketing. And, in any case, the founders also had a huge amount of social media presence, which was again zero-cost marketing.

Finally, Do You Have a Brand?

Aha. Brand. A most misused and maligned word. Let me tell you a story about A.C. Hathikhanawala, a sprightly young founder popularly known as Hathi (obviously, you wouldn't call him Sheru, would you?). Hathi had just launched a yummy chocolate called Chocoslim, which helped people lose weight. How? Well, when I met Hathi (that's right, I did have the honour of meeting him), he told me two things. First, these were low-calorie chocolates. But then so are many other low-calorie brands, isn't it? Big deal! No sir, these chocolates were special. Hathi's company had made them chewy, a bit like chewing gum. So, the calories expended in chewing and swallowing a bite of this chocolate were actually higher than the calories it contained. Therefore, with each bite of Chocoslim, you actually lost calories. And the more chocolates you ate, the more calories you lost, and therefore the slimmer you became.

Can you imagine what an earth-shattering product this was? Finally, mankind had discovered how to eat more and get slimmer. Finally, there was a yummy, tasty chocolate for those millions of human beings who were fighting a constant battle with their equator—in simple terms, their waistline. Yes sir, Hathi had hit upon just the right formula to permit people to continuously eat chocolates, and still maintain their respective waistlines at a slim and healthy forty-four inches.

However, my purpose here is not to sing eulogies about the product. It is to talk about the subject of brands. Sadly, therefore, we need to leave this fascinating subject. You see, wonderful though these chocolates were, they weren't really selling. Which is why Hathi had gone to his mentor for advice. Which mentor, did you ask? Come on, you know it. The bearded professor, of course!

After the usual coffee had been ordered, the first question the professor asked was, 'Hathi, there are lots of sugar-free sweets and chocolates available in the market. So why would anyone buy your stuff?'

Of course, Hathi had his answer well prepared, 'Well, first of all, my product is different. But even more important, most of the other stuff is unbranded, whereas my chocolates are branded. That's what people want.' And having said that, he sat back with a smug expression, as if to say, 'Come on, what a stupid question!'

But if you've met the bearded professor, you would have known that he was persistent. Very persistent. And so, he persisted, 'Hathi, I'd like to ask you a very simple question. What's a brand?'

Hathi looked surprised. 'Brand? Obvious, isn't it? The name under which I sell the product. In my case, Chocoslim. That's my brand.'

By now of course, the professor had realized the problem. 'Hathi, I agree that you've given your product a name—Chocoslim. But does that make it branded?'

Hathi looked at him as if he were a congenital idiot. 'Of course.'

'Hathi, you must understand the difference between a name and a brand. Right now, your chocolates have a name—Chocoslim. But not a brand. They will become a brand when your customers have heard about them. When they look at a packet on the shelf and say, "Ah, I've tried this brand earlier. It was tasty." When they talk about it and recommend it to their friends. That's a brand. And brands take time and money to build. When you give your product a name, that's only the first step in creating the brand. You need to make customers aware of it. And the more aware they are, the more your brand gets built.

'So, this is the critical part. Till your customer recognizes your brand, you are only a name. And for all practical purposes, you are unbranded. Which is why you've found it tough to sell.'

Hathi had a faraway look in his eyes as he heard out his mentor. He was thinking, 'You're probably right, sir. I never thought of this. I gave my product a name, but till the customer knows this name, and the fact that it's a high-quality product, it's just that—a name. Not a brand. So I guess, as I spend on advertising and marketing, and as more and more consumers buy it and perhaps even talk about it, the brand would start getting built. Till then, for all practical purposes, I have an unbranded product.'

'That's right. Remember, Hathi, you start with a name and build the brand over time.'

And Hathi broke out into a broad grin. 'Thank you, sir. You have really cleared up my fundas today. More coffee?'

So that was the meeting between Hathi and the bearded professor. But before I end, I'm sure you'd like to try out these wonderful chocolates that Hathi makes. And if, for some reason, you are not able to get them in the market, just send me an email along with a recent photograph. I have spoken to Hathi, and he has agreed to send free samples to you guys.

But only to deserving candidates!

16

The Business Plan

Welcome back, my friend. I'm sure you've lost a few milligrams after savouring those yummy Chocoslim chocolates. And now we need to get back to the second 'B' in our BOMB approach, where you put everything together in the form of a BUSINESS PLAN. That's right, a business plan is where everything comes together—your dream, the PERSISTENT business you are building, the wonderful team you plan to have in place and how you will execute your plans. So, let's take a look at this animal:

The Business Plan

In simple terms, a business plan is a document or a PowerPoint presentation that describes the key aspects of your business—what you plan to do and how you plan to do it. But why do you need this plan? Obvious, isn't it? After all, you've got to have a plan before you build your website. Or recruit people. Or splurge on marketing. In fact, before you do anything significant in your venture, you need to have a plan in place. And of course, if you are looking for funding, that's the first thing the investor will ask for.

Now this is extremely important, so please stop fiddling around with your phone and listen to me. The business plan is required for you as the founder, and also for the investor. Unfortunately, some founders believe that it is only needed when you are looking for money. And once you've got the money—well, its purpose is served, so you can dump it. No, my friend. You need a business plan to run your business successfully. Please get that into your head. And till you've done that, keep reading this paragraph again and again.

Obviously, the core of your business plan is a description of your business—which should ideally be a PERSISTENT business. But what else should it include? Well, first, you must list out your competitors, including potential competitors, where you stand compared to them, and how you will compete with them (remember the entry barrier in our PERSISTENT model?). And then of course, you must have a spreadsheet that contains your past revenues (traction in our PERSISTENT model) as well as costs. Along with reasonably detailed projections for the next twelve months, and a broader picture of the next couple of years. And yes, you must cover your unit economics.

Just to show you what these projections look like, let's go back to the story of Hathi and his wonderful product, Chocoslim, which you read about in the previous chapter. And let's assume for simplicity that Hathi was purely into online sales. He had a website where you could place your order and pay, and the company would deliver the appropriate number of packs to your home. In the following table, I've shown you what the business projections for the company would look like. You would normally show these projections for the period of a year, and after that, quarterly projections for the next couple of years. Of course, I have only shown you projections for six months, otherwise this book would have been perhaps two feet wide, and you would not have been able to fit it into your backpack. So, instead of cribbing, please thank me!

Business Projections for Chocoslim

	Month 1	Month 2	Month 3	Month 4	Month 5	Month 6
Revenues						
Number of packs sold	200	300	400	600	800	1,200
Total Revenues @ Rs 300 per pack	**60,000**	**90,000**	**1,20,000**	**1,80,000**	**2,40,000**	**3,60,000**
Direct Costs						
Production cost of packs sold @ Rs 100 per pack	20,000	30,000	40,000	60,000	80,000	1,20,000
Delivery cost @ Rs 50 per pack	10,000	15,000	20,000	30,000	40,000	60,000
Total Direct Costs	**30,000**	**45,000**	**60,000**	**90,000**	**1,20,000**	**1,80,000**
Indirect Costs						
Salaries	2,00,000	2,00,000	2,00,000	2,00,000	2,00,000	2,00,000
Marketing	1,00,000	1,00,000	1,00,000	2,00,000	2,00,000	2,00,000
Other Indirect Costs	1,00,000	1,00,000	1,00,000	1,00,000	1,00,000	1,00,000
Total Indirect Costs	**4,00,000**	**4,00,000**	**4,00,000**	**5,00,000**	**5,00,000**	**5,00,000**
Total Costs (Direct + Indirect)	**4,30,000**	**4,45,000**	**4,60,000**	**5,90,000**	**6,20,000**	**6,80,000**
Cash Inflow (Total Revenues minus Total Costs)	**-3,70,000**	**-3,55,000**	**-3,40,000**	**-4,10,000**	**-3,80,000**	**-3,20,000**
Cumulative Cash Inflow	**-3,70,000**	**-7,25,000**	**-10,65,000**	**-14,75,000**	**-18,55,000**	**-21,75,000**

While on the subject of projections, there is something important that you must remember. When you are at an early stage, your projections can go haywire. They could easily be far too low, or far too high. Simply because everything is experimental at this stage. Over time of course, once the business begins to stabilize, they will get closer and closer to actuals. But what is critical is the assumptions you are making, and the basis for these assumptions. In the case of Chocoslim, for instance, would Hathi put up huge hoardings outside all weight-reducing clinics? Would he appoint dieticians as his brand ambassadors? Would he be part of social media groups that focused on the mythical subject of weight reduction? You see? Numbers alone are not enough. You need to be clear about how you will achieve them.

Now, I must bring in another commonly used term in the world of start-ups. You see, at the next party you must impress the girls (or boys, depending on your gender). Take a look at the second-last row in this table. You would notice that for each of the months I have shown, you have negative cash flow. This means that you are spending more than you are earning. And that, ladies and gentlemen, is also called cash burn, because you are burning up whatever cash you have. And this cash burn stops when your monthly revenues start exceeding your monthly costs.

Clear?

Ask and Runway

Finally, there are two more figures that need to go into the business plan. Let's get back to Chocoslim's business projections. Take a look at the last row, which shows you the cumulative cash flow for this company—also called cumulative burn in case it is negative. Now let's assume the company had Rs 15 lakh in the bank at the start of the first month. How long would that last? Four months, isn't it? Because till the fourth month, the cumulative burn would be Rs 14.75 lakh. But after that, there would be no money left. In the world of start-ups, we say that the runway for this company is four months.

Why the term runway? Well, you are familiar with the runway at an airport. The crucial issue here is that an aircraft can only taxi as far as the runway. Before the runway ends, it needs to take off. In the same way, the money you have in the bank gives you a runway. And before you come to the end of this runway, your business must take off—in other words, become profitable. If it doesn't, well, you'll need funding to extend the runway.

And now for a practical tip. It's a good idea to have a runway of at least twelve months. Because if you don't, you will soon run out of money and will constantly be in fundraising mode. And therefore, you won't have time to focus on managing and growing the business. In the case of Chocoslim, let's assume that the cumulative burn at the end of twelve months is Rs 35 lakh. That means the company requires Rs 35 lakh to last out these twelve months. Of this amount, they already have Rs 15 lakh in the bank. Therefore, they need an additional funding of Rs 20 lakh. And that, ladies and gentlemen, is the 'Ask'. In other words, the amount of funding needed from investors.

And since this is important, I've put it down as a formula:

'Ask' = 'Cumulative burn' at the end of the 'runway' minus 'current bank balance'

Another question. What if the cash flow turns positive at some stage—say, in month eight? Well then, you only need funding to take care of your burn till that stage. Because after that, your business itself will generate the money you need. However, just keep in mind the fact that things can go wrong. Horribly wrong. Therefore, it's a good idea to ask for funding for at least a few months beyond this point—just to be safe.

Typically, an early-stage start-up can ask for anywhere between Rs 50 lakh and a few crores, depending on the state of the business—especially the traction. Of course, you would also need to tell the investors what you plan to do with this money. No investor will part with his hard-earned money till he knows exactly what it will be used for.

And with that, my friend, your business plan is complete. Now you are all set to get those fresh, crisp currency notes. Actually it's not really currency notes, but something more boring—money in your bank account.

That's right. You now need to meet investors. In the next chapter . . .

17

Angels, VCs and Other Animals

And now for the big stuff. You've created your business plan. And you find that you need funding. Which means that you need to approach investors.

But who are these guys? Who are angel investors? And who are VCs or venture capitalists? Yes, sir, if you need funding, you'll need to understand a bit about these animals . . .

By the way, I've mentioned earlier that I have written another book on the specific subject of funding, along with my close friend and co-author, Sushanto Mitra. It's called *Funding Your Start-Up: And Other Nightmares.* Obviously, you'll get many more details about investors and funding—and more cases—there. But I've included a summary in this chapter just in case the other book is sold out 😊!

The 'Family and Friends' Round

When you start your company, you would obviously need to dip into your savings—assuming of course that you do not have the lavish Vijay Mallya kind of lifestyle. And then you start running the company, but soon discover that your savings are not enough and you need to go elsewhere. Where to? Well, your father for a start. Or your father in-law, if you have the misfortune of being married. Or like Akela and Dukela in chapter 5, you might even go to your rich chacha or mama and beg for money. By the way, I would strongly advise you to maintain good relations with all your rich relatives. Wish them on their birthday, on Diwali, on Eid, on Christmas, on New Year's Day. In fact, create opportunities to wish them. Try it. It doesn't take much effort. And some day you'll thank me for the advice. Because you never know when you might need their money (of course, you can also wish your poorer relatives, but that's up to you). In addition, you can approach your friends—again, those who do not follow the Vijay Mallya school of spending. So that's the first round of funding—the family and friends round.

The important thing to note here, is that these friends and relatives know you, and therefore, there is some level of trust. At least I hope so. If not, you must have done something terribly wrong. So, those who do put in their money are likely to do so at a fairly early stage in your journey, well before you have built your product. Definitely well before you have started getting revenues. And they are not likely to ask too many questions. In fact, they might even say something like, '*Beta, mujhe pata hai tu nalaayak hai. Par apna bachcha hai. Le le do lakh* (Son, I know you are useless. But you are my nephew. Here, take two lakhs).' In other words, these people are willing to take a risk with you. But because your start-up is completely unproven and the risk is high, the amount of money they put in is likely to be fairly low. Unless, of course, you have the good fortune of having been born into the Tata or Ambani family. Typically, the total amount raised through friends and family is likely to be less than Rs 20 lakh, but, of course, this is a ballpark figure.

However, you soon run out of money. And, by now, it has become embarrassing to approach your chacha and mama again. In any case, you've also discovered that their birthdays are at least eight months away, whereas you need the money now! So, who do you go to?

Angel investors, of course!

Angel Investors

Angel investors—or simply angels—are the first external investors in your business. What do I mean by external? Those who don't know you! And therefore, unlike your friends and family, they will not invest right in the beginning of your journey. Instead, they will wait for the business to stabilize a bit. And, of course, they would need to understand it in far greater detail than your friends and family would. On the other hand, they invest more. Typically, an angel round can be anywhere between Rs 50 lakh and Rs 4 crore, but, once again, these are ballpark figures.

One important issue. How do you locate angel investors? Let's say you go on to the road, stop the first Mercedes-Benz you see and ask the person sitting inside, 'Sir, are you an angel investor?' And, of course, he glares at you and turns up the window. But you are a DREAM Founder and highly persevering, so you try the next car—a Jaguar this time. This guy is a bit more polite, but it turns out that he only invests in real estate—because of the colour of his money, you see? Over time, you get more and more frustrated because you are not able to find an angel investor.

But you never realized that he's right there—your next-door neighbour, who dresses shabbily and drives a Maruti.

You see? Locating an angel investor is not easy. It's not written on their face.

So, how do you find them?

Aha. The answer is, you don't!

You don't? But then how do you get their money?

My friend, I told you, you don't locate angel investors. You locate an angel network instead.

Angel network? What's this new animal?

Actually it's fairly simple. An angel network is like a club, where each member is an angel investor. So, you approach an angel network for funding, and not the individual member. If they like your business—and perhaps your face—they ask you to pitch the idea to their members. And if the members also like your business and your face, well, you've got your money!

How do you locate angel networks? Well, there are a few large ones such as Indian Angel Network, Lead Angels, Chennai Angels and Mumbai Angels. And some smaller, local ones like Chandigarh Angels and Jaipur Angels. All you need to do is to run to Google, which will give you their websites and email IDs. And you can apply for funding over there!

Agreed? So, you apply to an angel network, and you get their angel money. Armed with this unexpected windfall, you first go to the bar to celebrate, of course. And then you happily splurge. And splurge some more. And some more . . .

Till you run out of the money you got! But you still need more. And whom do you go to now? VCs, of course.

Venture Capitalists

I'm sure you've heard the term venture capitalist, or VC. But do you know the fundamental difference between an angel and a VC? No? OK, let me take a parallel from the stock market. You see, there are two ways in which you can invest in the stock market. A savvy investor would study potential companies, and then take a decision to invest in a particular company, say, Reliance Industries. On the other hand, you might be an investor who wants to make money in the stock market, but doesn't have the time or the knowhow to study potential companies. What would you do in such a case? Invest in a mutual fund, of course! Where you hand over your money to the fund manager, who in turn invests it in specific companies such as Reliance or Hindustan Unilever on your behalf. And this is the HUGE difference between the two situations. In the first case, you invest your own money, whereas in the second case, the fund manager invests your money on your behalf.

It's exactly the same with angels and VCs: angels invest their own money, whereas VCs invest other people's money. In other words, VCs act like mutual fund managers. They float a fund, and potential investors invest in this fund. And then these VCs proceed to invest this money on behalf of their investors.

And now you can see how this makes a difference. Since the VC is investing someone else's money, he cannot take the kind of risks that the angel can. Which means that he will usually invest at a later stage compared to angels—when the business is more stable and proven. Obviously, at this later stage, the valuation would have gone up, but that's okay with the VC. And, I almost forgot—the VC will usually invest far more money than angels can. Typically, around Rs 4 crore or more. Or if you find dollars more exciting, half a million dollars and above.

We have lots of VCs in the market today, looking for those juicy investments. Sequoia Capital, SAIF Partners, Tiger Global Management, SoftBank, Chiratae Ventures and Lightspeed Venture Partners are just some of them.

So, you've now met angel investors and you've met VCs. But you also need to understand what these two look for, before they make an investment.

What Do Investors Look For?

Aha. That's a million-dollar question. Let's start with angel investors; we'll talk about VCs later. First of all, what does the angel want out of an investment? Why is he putting in hard-earned money (or the windfall he got from his parents. It doesn't matter which)? Very simply, he hopes to grow his investment and ultimately get an exit. In other words, he buys a certain number of shares in the company, and after a few years, hopes to sell them to another investor. At a higher price or valuation—if you prefer the term. Something that we call an exit.

But the second investor will buy these shares only if the company has been successful. After all, who invests in a failure? So what are the factors that lead to success? Well, the company should be solving a problem for some customer. Its customers should be willing to pay for the solution. In other words, the company should have an earnings model, the market size should be large, and the company should show significant traction by scaling up rapidly.

Sounds familiar? Of course it does! For the company to be successful, it should follow the PERSISTENT model, shouldn't it? And who leads the company to success? A DREAM Founder, of course!

Next question. What about VCs? Actually, their requirements are fairly similar, aren't they? Just like angels, they would also like to invest in a successful, growing company, so that they in turn can sell their shares to a VC in future at a higher valuation. And therefore, get an exit. The only difference of course, is that VCs expect far more traction, and therefore invest at a later stage. Of course, they will study the company in a lot more depth than the typical angel investor would. After all, they are putting in much more money—and that too, money that belongs to someone else.

So that's it. Both angel investors and VCs look for DREAM Founders and PERSISTENT businesses to invest in. Please remember that when you go in for fundraising.

Strategic Investors

Now, this is a completely different kind of investor, and the last kind that we'll talk about. Let's take the example of Ghotala Bank, one of the largest and most respected banks in the country.

The bank gives loans to its customers for buying homes, cars, motorbikes, yachts, villas, etc. But it doesn't give you loans for buying cows, or buffaloes, or goats, or chickens. For multiple reasons. First of all, the amount involved is too small (at least I think so. I have never bought a buffalo, so I really don't know what it would cost). And secondly, these transactions take place in villages, where a lot of the dealings are in cash. So, Ghotala Bank happily skips buffalo loans.

However, in one of their board meetings, the management decided that the bank was missing out a huge opportunity by not looking at buffalo loans. A massive growth area, in spite of all the vegans out there. The problem of course, was that Ghotala Bank did not understand this area. And in any case, the overheads of giving out such small loans were too high.

But there was a brilliant solution. You have probably heard the term microfinance. Microfinance companies give low-value loans to rural women, to start or expand small businesses. This could be for buying chickens, or cows, or buffaloes, or even for setting up small shops in their homes. Now, microfinance is a fascinating subject and I would have loved to go on and on about it. But my editor, Radhika, wisely told me to hold on to the subject for a future book.

Anyhow, BhainsaLoan (buffalo loan, for those who don't understand Hindi) was one such microfinance company. The founders had successfully grown their business but were now looking for more funding. And just by chance, the founder of BhainsaLoan and the CEO of Ghotala Bank happened to meet at a conference.

So, what do you think happened? Simple. Ghotala Bank wanted to enter the microfinance business but didn't know how to. And BhainsaLoan needed money. So, Ghotala Bank happily invested in BhainsaLoan and acquired 20 per cent equity in the company. A true win-win, wasn't it?

And now for the crucial bit. Why did Ghotala Bank invest in BhainsaLoan? Was it to get an exit? Of course not. The bank invested in the microfinance company because it was an interesting extension to their current business. They took a 20 per cent stake to try it out, but if things worked out, they were quite prepared to buy out BhainsaLoan completely. So, their interest was strategic and very long-term. And that, my friend, is a strategic investor—a company that invests in another company because they feel it's a good add-on to their existing business, and not to get an exit. Unlike angels and VCs, who are pure financial investors and whose aim is to enter at a certain valuation, and to ultimately exit at a higher valuation. And, by the way, that's one more term you have learnt to throw around at your next party ☺.

So that's it. These are the three kinds of investors you are likely to meet when you raise funds.

And now it's time for some more stories. Stories of successful start-ups as well as failures. Which we will analyse using the two frameworks you have learnt, namely, DREAM Founder and PERSISTENT Business.

In the next section . . .

Let's Meet Annurag Batra, chairman and editor-in-chief, *BW Businessworld*, and founder, exchange4media group

When you think of business magazines and 360-degree business media platforms, which is the first one that comes to mind? *BW Businessworld*, of course. Headed by the hugely energetic, forever gung-ho chairman and chief editor, Annurag Batra. Annurag has been a highly successful serial entrepreneur, and has also founded the exchange4media group. But of course, you know all this. What you probably do not know is that Annurag was part of the first batch of MBA students at MDI. And even though I joined MDI as a professor a few years later, I've often had the privilege of sharing chai and samosas with him at the wonderful open-air canteen at MDI. It has always been great fun and a major learning experience talking to Annurag. Which is why, when I decided to write this book, I simply had to get his views. And this is what he told me—over the inevitable chai, of course:

> The starting point for any DREAM Founder is obvious. He needs to be a big dreamer. Think big. Be willing to take risks. Take leaps of faith. Think differently. Challenge conventional wisdom. Look at the big guys around you, whether it is Sanjeev Bikhchandani of Naukri, Byju Ravindran of Byju's, Deep Kalra of MakeMyTrip, or any of the other success stories in India. They all dreamt big and look where they have reached.
>
> But of course, dreaming alone will not get you anywhere. You've got to translate it into reality. And for that, you need to keep a few things in mind. First of all, you must be a long-term player. Creating your business is not a two-year job. It's a lifelong commitment. And you'll definitely have challenges along the way.

Be resilient in the face of these challenges. Don't give up. Keep at it, think long term, and hopefully you'll be able to overcome them.

And then you need to have the ability to build teams. You cannot do everything yourself. You need the support of people with diverse skills. People you can rely on. People you can trust. Empower your guys, allow them space to work and to grow, develop them. And build your business along with them.

Of course, you need to have the ability to raise funds and then use them to scale rapidly. Scaling your business is critical to survival—because if you don't scale, your competitor will, he will eat into your market share, and ultimately kill you. As a DREAM Founder therefore, you need to scale before the other guy can.

One final comment. A DREAM Founder needs to be supported by dream partners, whether they are co-founders, investors or advisers. And of course, a dream team of employees.

In my opinion, these are a few of the critical issues you must take care of in building a successful business. And with this, let me wish all of you young founders all the very best of luck.

Thanks a lot, Annurag. I'm sure our readers would find your advice extremely useful. And I hope to have many, many more chai-samosa meetings with you in the open-air canteen at MDI.

Section IV

Those Who Succeeded and Those Who Didn't

18

Those Yummy Desi Candies from GO DESi

By now you have learnt all about the frameworks I had to share. Now, let's apply our learning to some more start-ups and their founders. Starting with those that succeeded.

And I can't think of a better way to begin than by telling you the fascinating story of GO DESi. Our story begins in the month of January 2018. Vinay Kothari was trekking in the Western Ghats in Karnataka, when he happened to walk up to a small kirana shop. Among other things, he noticed that the shop was selling locally made candies. Curious, Vinay tried one. It was made of katthal (jackfruit for those who don't understand Hindi) and it was yummy. And then he noticed some more varieties—there was imli (tamarind), kaccha aam (raw mango), khatta nimbu (sour lemon) and a host of others. Completely unbranded, of course, but extremely tasty. Vinay was intrigued. As a kid he had had candy which was orange, lemon or strawberry flavoured, but those were all based on synthetic flavours. But here he had katthal, imli and kaccha aam, which he had never had before. And they all seemed to be completely natural. No synthetic flavours.

Barely able to contain his excitement, Vinay asked the shopkeeper where these were made, and he was directed to a small village nearby. Yes, you heard right—a village in rural Karnataka. Within minutes, Vinay changed course (remember, he was on a trek) and started off for this village. Having asked for directions from a few villagers, he landed up at the candy-making 'factory'. Actually a small shed, which we will call a micro-unit. The owner was a farmer, who grew the fruit that was ultimately converted to candies in this micro-unit. Extremely courteous, he even treated Vinay to a huge glass of fresh, creamy, frothy buffalo milk, which Vinay—polite person that he was—could not refuse.

During the next few hours, Vinay understood how the farmer (we'll call him a micro-entrepreneur) was making these desi candies. He realized that the farmer was not using any artificial flavouring or preservatives. In fact, he wasn't even using sugar, preferring to use gur, or jaggery, instead—nothing that could make his candy the least bit unhealthy. Excitement at a fever pitch by now, Vinay desperately managed to drain his third glass of buffalo milk and left for home.

Over the next few days he was in a daze. But of course, you wouldn't know why, so let me give you a bit of background. You see, after his MBA, Vinay had worked in ITC for seven years. But now, as it happens with many of us, the entrepreneurship bug had begun to bite (we call it *keeda* in Hindi. And *poka* in Bengali. And I'm sure there are equivalents in Tamil and Telugu. But whatever the language, I'm sure you get what I mean. It's a bug, and once you've got it, well, you've got it. And you cannot escape from it). Vinay realized that he simply had to start something on his own. That much was clear. But what? That was not clear!

However, things began to change on that fateful day when he visited the candy-making unit in rural Karnataka. He realized that there were lots of different kinds of sweets and candies available in the market but none which were typically Indian. Moreover, most of these had lots of (ugh) synthetic flavours and preservatives. And plenty of sugar—which, as you are aware, is a no-no these days. The candy he had tasted had no preservatives, no synthetic additives, no added colour, and was made using jaggery instead of sugar. In simple terms, it had a yummy but different taste, and it was healthy as well. What a deadly combination!

Of course, as you can imagine, there were problems. Two in particular. Firstly, these were unbranded candies. And if you happen to live in a city or even a smaller town, you would realize the importance of branding, especially in foodstuffs. People prefer branded stuff even if it means paying more (remember our discussion on branding in chapter 15?). Secondly, there was no real distribution network for these candies, which is why they were only available around the village where they were manufactured. But this is where Vinay came in. He had spent time in sales and distribution in the food and agri-business divisions of ITC. And he had travelled within different states of the country. As a consequence, he understood both branded foods, and sales and distribution. The micro-entrepreneur would make the candy, and Vinay would brand it and sell it through a distribution network. The size of the market was huge (remember our PERSISTENT framework?). No, it was HUGE. And completely untapped. And Vinay, along with lots of farmers, would make these natural, healthy sweets with Indian flavours available to the entire country. That was his dream.

That's where Vinay had his next brainwave. Why not use the brand name 'GO DESi?' It conveyed everything that he wanted the brand to. Within that, each product would use the 'DESi' sub-brand. And that's how DESi POPz lollipops were launched in April 2018. When Vinay booked a stall in a flea market in Bangalore. And guess what happened? The stall had been booked for three days, but the stocks were sold out within the first morning itself. And by the way, the excitement level in his family was so high that his sister, Raksha, decided to join him as co-founder.

By now Vinay realized that he had struck gold. All he needed was a shovel to collect it. Using all his experience in setting up distribution networks, he then started supplying these lollipops to local retail stores. And guess who delivered stocks to these retailers?

Vinay on his sister's bike! To cut down costs. By the way, this simple action gives you a peek into Vinay's attitude. That's right. He was willing to do everything. And show the way to his team!

The next step, of course, was e-commerce—in other words, selling these candies online. Which meant two things. First, the founders had to create their own website, where customers could buy these candies. Also, they tied up with partners for deliveries. Secondly, they had to make these products available on the giant e-commerce sites, namely Amazon and Flipkart. They did both, and business began to pick up. No, it began to roar . . .

However, somewhere along the line, there was a problem. And I'm sure you can guess what it was. You see, the micro-unit that was making these candies could not scale up (remember our PERSISTENT model, where I had told you that scaling up was critical, otherwise competitors could get in and capture the market?). Try as he might, the farmer simply couldn't scale up fast enough. And therefore, that huge, wonderful market, which was just waiting to be grabbed, remained elusive.

Now, what would you have done in this situation? Come on, tell me—you are a founder too, aren't you? Well, the opportunity was huge, but the partner wasn't able to scale up. So, Vinay decided to understand the whole issue of scalability, by building the product himself (the 'B' in our BOMB model). Therefore, he set up his own unit, with a much higher capacity than the one the farmer was running. With that, he was able to scale up rapidly. In fact, within just a couple of years of starting off, he had a thousand retail outlets in Bangalore. And online sales boomed as well, with ten thousand orders per month on his own GO DESi website, and another ten thousand orders per month on Amazon.

But there is something else that happened. And I don't want to steal Vinay's thunder, so let's hear him out:

We realized that we were in a cottage industry. And for such businesses to scale, it was vital to standardize processes. All the way from sourcing raw materials, to preparing and packaging the final product, ready for dispatch. The purpose of setting up our own unit was to do exactly this—understand and standardize these processes, and therefore make the business scalable.

So, Vinay had set up his own unit, with a higher capacity than those of his micro-entrepreneurs. And was therefore able to scale the business. But to scale even beyond this, he would need to add more units. And that would mean land, money, infrastructure and people. Which meant that scalability would get hit once again. However, Vinay was smart. Rather than adding more units on his own, he went scouting for new partners—farmers who could think long-term, and were willing to invest in capacity. These farmers became micro-entrepreneurs for GO DESi as before. And now that processes had been standardized, well, it was easier for each of them to scale.

But there was one more extremely important reason to add partners, rather than adding his own units. Let's hear out Vinay, once again:

> We realized that consumer companies needed to continuously innovate and add great products, in order to grow. For this, we had two options. One was to have our own R&D team, which would work on creating such products. But that would only be able to create a limited number of new products. A far better option was to go out and locate micro-entrepreneurs *who had already developed wonderful products*, and were manufacturing them. Of course, these guys had to have the desire and vision to scale. These micro-entrepreneurs became our partners, and were therefore part of our extended R&D team. Having got such people on board, we would apply all our learning and help them to standardize their processes. And finally, market their products under our umbrella brand, GO DESi.

Dear reader, I want you to pause for a moment and think. When scalability became an issue, can you see how Vinay streamlined his operations? First, he set up his own unit to understand and standardize processes. And then he went out to onboard micro-entrepreneurs. All the while helping them to implement the processes that he had standardized. And boy, was he successful? At the time of writing this book, he had roped in five farmers who had set up micro-units in Karnataka. And thanks to them, he has expanded his product range well beyond imli and jackfruit lollipops. He now has DESi Chaat, DESi Meetha, DESi Mints and much more. And, of course, business has continued to boom!

Now there is something very, very, very, very important that I have to tell you, so please pay attention and listen (by the way, I thought of adding a few more 'verys' just to ensure that you got the message. But my editor Radhika felt that four 'verys' were enough. Can't waste paper, you see?). Remember, when I spoke about DREAM Founders, I had told you that you needed to build the right team? Now, your team is not just your employees. It includes your partners, distributors and your retailers as well. In this case, the micro-entrepreneurs were Vinay's partners, and therefore very much a part of his team. And notice what Vinay had done. Early on in the journey of GO DESi, he realized that there was a huge demand for his DESi products. The only constraint was the processing capacity. Which meant that as partners, he needed to get in farmers who themselves had the vision and the willingness to scale. In addition to being quality conscious, of course. And that's exactly what he did. He began looking for such potential micro-entrepreneurs who then joined his team.

But there is more. As you are aware, putting the right team together is only the first step. You also need to develop them, help them to grow, and ultimately turn them into happy, long-term members of your team. But how? Let's digress for a bit. Remember, GO DESi was into the processed foods industry. In this industry, the usual practice is that the farmer grows the vegetables or fruit, and then hands it over to a factory for processing. As an example, the farmer might grow potatoes, and then sell them to a processing unit that makes potato chips. *Importantly, the farmer does not process the potatoes himself.* And therefore, he earns only around 10 per cent of what the consumer pays for the chips. But now, *Vinay had got the farmer himself to process his fruit and vegetables.* No need for an additional processing unit. Therefore, the farmer got a far bigger share of the pie—around 30 per cent of what the consumer paid. By the way, Vinay also decided to subsidize those farmers who needed help to stay afloat, at least in the beginning. He was building long-term partnerships, you see? And I must tell you something—all his partner micro-entrepreneurs are profitable today.

And were these micro-entrepreneurs happy? You bet! From 10 per cent to 30 per cent was a huge jump. They were absolutely delighted and became permanent team members for GO DESi. In other words, not only was Vinay running a flourishing business, he was also furthering a social cause by enabling farmers to get far more for their produce. In addition to generating employment in rural areas. You see, Vinay has a mantra for this venture—'Eat Good, Do Good'. And you can see this mantra playing out in whatever he does.

What about funding? Well, investors have lapped up his story. At the time of writing this book, GO DESi had already raised two rounds—Rs 1 crore in 2018 from Lead Angels and others, and subsequently funding of over Rs 7 crore from Rukam Capital and a few other investors.

But there is something else that I must tell you. As you are aware by now (and I hope you are), to be a true DREAM Founder, you need to make opportunities out of crises. And no crisis could be bigger than the Covid pandemic that hit the country in early 2020, and the subsequent lockdown. Most businesses were hit, and GO DESi was no different. However, Vinay was smart. He realized that he could take advantage of the way in which he had structured his operations. Let's see how.

You see, he was in the food processing industry, where agricultural produce would typically be picked up from farmers, transported to processing units, and then processed to make the final product. Now, the lockdown had hit two things. First of all, most of his competitors had supply chains that were geographically spread out. So in many cases, the farmer and the processing unit were located in different states. And, as you are aware, interstate transportation of goods was badly affected by the lockdown. But Vinay's supply chain, from the farmer to the processing unit, was entirely within the state of Karnataka, and was therefore not really impacted. Further, many competitors had their processing units in cities or towns, where the lockdown was most severe. But GO DESi had its units in rural areas, which had largely been spared the vicious Covid wave.

This meant that Vinay could go all out and grab market share from his competitors. All that he required was permission from the local authorities. And with that, he swung into action. He chased the local government officials for all he was worth and managed to get them to agree. Within a month, his business was back to pre-Covid levels. And yes, he had significantly increased market share during the crisis.

But there's something more, so do read on. During the lockdown, people were forced to stay at home. And, of course, you know what they did—they spent all those frustrating hours on the Internet, consuming content. And that's where Vinay had a brainwave. Why not provide them with content that would build his brand? Which is exactly what he did. He started a page on Facebook and Instagram called DESi *Nukkad* (nukkad in Hindi means street corner) where he provided lots of content on yoga and mental health, as well as other natural approaches to remaining healthy. All within the ambit of 'DESi'. And boy, did people consume his content? Sitting at home, desperate to find ways to cope with the lockdown, they were all too keen. When the lockdown gradually lifted, sales boomed. At the time of writing this book, DESi POPz had become the fastest-selling confectionery brand on Amazon! That's the success story of GO DESi. And the brand is now Vinay's biggest entry barrier for competition!

Finally, if you were to visit Bangalore today, you are welcome to meet Vinay. I can do the introductions.

But I must tell you, it's unlikely that you'll catch him there. More likely, he will be in some village in Karnataka. Roping in yet another happy micro-entrepreneur.

19

Jab Belita Met Enrich

This is the story of Garima Jain. Young, married and in a corporate job in the city of Mumbai. And like many others in her position, struggling to find time to go to a beauty parlour. The job was demanding, the timings were long and the traffic was . . . well, it was Mumbai traffic. Need I say more? Slow and never-ending. And that's why Garima invariably reached home tired. Going to the parlour on her way home from office was simply not an option. After a long day, she just wanted to reach home. And then, of course, weekends were full of chores which all of us know so well.

Sure, there was advice galore from her friends. 'Why don't you call a beautician home? There are so many of them who will come home and give you a facial. Or anything else you want.' But I'm sure you can guess what Garima's response was. 'Yuck. Most of them are so unprofessional. No way.' And that was that. As life carried on—minus parlours!

But one fine day something happened, which was to change this forever. On that day, Garima had had a particularly long day at the office. And thanks to one of the frequent repair jobs that Mumbai roads are so fond of, she was even more tired than normal. She flopped down on the sofa, took a couple of deep breaths and said, 'I need a pizza to recover from today.' Her husband Akshay, who was a graduate from IIT Madras and a ship designer by profession, took the hint and ordered pizza on the phone. While Garima dozed off . . .

But not for long. Garima woke up with a start, because the pizza was in her hands in less than half an hour. It was one of the well-known brands; hot, completely standard and hygienically packed. And while sinking her teeth into it, she said, 'This is great. Yummy, hot, standardized stuff. Clean, hygienic, and you know just what you are getting.' But the next remark was the real killer. With a faraway, dreamy look in her eyes, she said, 'I wish we could get beauty treatment at home in the same way—standardized, clean, hygienic . . .'

With that casual remark, Garima carried on munching. But Akshay stopped. Pizza suspended in mid-air, around two inches from his waiting teeth. And with a strange look in his eyes, he said, 'Why don't you start it?'

Dear reader, that half hour in the Jain household would go on to change the world. Well, that's not strictly correct. But it would definitely change Garima and Akshay's world. And the world of lots and lots of women in the city of Mumbai. Because that's where the idea for Belita was born. Suddenly the pizza was forgotten, as both husband and wife looked at each other, 'Why not?'

With that, the young couple swung into action. Their idea was simple and yet powerful. The beauty business in India had enormous potential—after all, which woman would not want to improve her looks? But many of them might not be keen to go to a parlour. Just consider a few situations: A lady had a terrific party to attend at night, where everyone else would be absolutely tip-top—straight from the parlour. There was no way this lady could attend the party without a stint at the parlour. But what if it were horribly hot and muggy during the day? Or what if it were raining cats and dogs—and perhaps mice as well? Or what if it was sheer inertia? And therefore—heaven forbid—what if this poor lady were to land up at the party without that mandatory visit? She would be the topic of conversation among her friends for days, if not weeks, wouldn't she?

But what was the option? Call a beautician home, naturally. But most of these people were unprofessional and completely untrained. In simple Hindi, *jugaadu* (a makeshift person). And worst of all, the jars of cream and other stuff they used would probably be re-used repeatedly. Just imagine, the beautician would keep dipping her finger into a jar, apply the cream on to the skin of one customer, close the jar at the end of the process, and voila—the same jar with whatever had been transferred from this customer's skin would be used for the next customer. How appetizing!

Akshay and Garima realized that the size of the market for beauty treatment at home was immense. Women were desperately waiting for a trusted, professional organization which would provide these services in a standardized, hygienic way. And that was the dream of our young couple—to provide trusted, hygienic, professional beauty services at home to every Indian woman! Which is how they launched 'Belita—Salon Comes Home'. By the way, in case you are familiar with Spanish, you would know that 'belita' in Spanish means beautiful.

They decided to start in the city that they were familiar with, namely Mumbai, a huge market in itself. And I must tell you something really interesting that happened next. Initially, Akshay's role was simply to support Garima in the project. But over time he got so excited, that he stopped designing ships and moved into the project full-time. Of course, the fact that he was dealing with beautiful women here had nothing to do with his decision 😊!

Having decided on the name, Akshay and Garima went about the tough part of making the business more professional. And they realized that execution was the key. Specifically operations. First of all, they decided on smart, clean uniforms for the beauticians they sent to customers' homes, so that they stood out from the local beauticians. Over time, the customer would see this as a part of the Belita brand. Secondly, they decided to use disposable jars of cream and other products. In other words, they would use small jars of cream (or sachets), each of which was used for only one customer. After the session was over, this jar was thrown away, and a brand new jar would be opened for the next customer. So, the dirty 'customer to customer transfer' was avoided. Of course, this implied slightly higher costs, but they figured—quite rightly— that customers would be willing to pay.

Training was the other key activity for Belita. This was handled by Garima. An intensive training programme was designed and implemented, so that all beauticians followed exactly the same processes and used exactly the same products in their treatment. Something like the McDonald's model, where a chicken burger (sorry vegetarians—the same would apply to a veg burger as well) would taste the same, no matter which outlet you went to, and what the parentage of the chicken (or potato) was.

Akshay and Garima then created a website where customers could figure out the services available, along with corresponding prices—whether it was waxing or facials or anything else (you would appreciate that, as a male, I am not aware of too many terms in this business, but you get the idea, don't you?). Customers could then book an appointment, and a well-trained, smartly uniformed beautician from Belita would come over to their home at the appointed time. In addition, Akshay created an app for customers to be used for the same purpose. And, of course, if you wanted, you could always book an appointment on the phone.

And finally, the logistics. Let's hear Akshay on this subject:

We decided to create hubs scattered across Mumbai, where the beauticians would be based. All products to be used would also be kept in these hubs. Importantly, these hubs were air-conditioned, so as to avoid sweaty beauticians. Further, we had air-conditioned vans to transport beauticians to various customers, once again for the same reason. And therefore, the customer got a professionally trained beautician, smartly turned out in uniform, with fresh products to be used and the remainder disposed of. Which is just what the customer wanted!

Of course, our founders needed money to fund all this. For which they approached angel investors. Fortunately, the angels bought the concept immediately. Predominantly male, most of them married, all of them were aware of the regular visits their wives made to the neighbourhood parlour. And the cribs and complaints when they had to go in the sun or rain, or when they were tired, or when . . .

But you get the idea. The angels were delighted, and Belita was able to raise not just one but two rounds of funding in quick succession. With these funds Akshay and Garima added more hubs, and went all out to grow their market. All in Mumbai—they were clear that this was a large enough market and there was no need to spread themselves thin by getting into new cities. Yes, there was competition, but there was enough business for everyone. They also expanded into the marriage market, where Belita's beauticians were available for wedding functions. In fact, very soon they had a significant 3000 appointments per month. Of course, this was a highly seasonal market, but so what? As long as business was flowing in, things were hunky-dory.

Well, not quite. If you've been reading this story carefully, you would remember that Belita's operational expenses were quite significant. For instance, the cost of renting the hubs as well as the marketing expenses were just too high. Akshay and Garima realized fairly soon that these overheads were unsustainable. It was becoming a crisis. And that's where they had their second brainwave. You see, both husband and wife were DREAM

Founders, and their thinking was highly flexible. They realized that a change was needed, and they were more than willing to make that change. They figured out that they could share these overheads by merging their company with a chain of physical beauty parlours. Potentially, it would be a win-win for both. Training and marketing could be common for both. Some of Belita's hubs—those that were doing well—could continue as they were. Others could be merged with the existing beauty parlours, with no separate rentals or maintenance. Even some of the beauticians could be common. And with the overheads reduced, Belita would be on the path to growth once again.

Interestingly, they did find such a chain—Enrich Salon, the well-known chain of parlours in Mumbai and elsewhere. Vikram Bhatt, the dynamic founder of Enrich, saw the synergies in the merger. He realized that with this merger, Enrich could span the entire beauty space—and not just physical beauty parlours. The rest, as they say, is history. Belita was acquired by Enrich, and the shareholders of the erstwhile Belita got shares in Enrich instead (if you recall our discussions in chapter 17, Enrich became a strategic investor in Belita). Garima joined Enrich, and Akshay went back to designing ships.

One last comment. This was an interesting case of a husband-wife team of founders. Both highly experienced, knowledgeable and focused. A terrific combination, provided of course, that they were able to work together. Which, in this case, they certainly were (the married reader would probably be in complete disagreement with this statement, but let's leave that subject for another book).

Anyhow, the business is now chugging along nicely, apart from the usual Covid hiccups, of course.

Now, dear reader, if you live in Mumbai, or plan to visit the city sometime, do let me know. I can talk to Vikram and get you a facial—or any other service from Enrich.

In fact, I might even be able to get you a discount . . .

20

Lots of Suggestions but No Funding

Okay guys, we've seen and analysed several start-ups that succeeded. But now it's important to look at a few that failed. For a start, let's meet Rangaswamy Kuppuswamy Palinipathy Parathasarathy S. Iyer. No one had quite figured out what the 'S' in Ranga's name stood for. Anyhow, that should not concern us. What should concern us is Ranga's problem. You see, he had spent a few years with a couple of leading multinationals in Bangalore. Money was no issue, along with whatever money could buy. But there was something missing. Life was strangely empty. And Ranga could not quite place it. Don't get me wrong. He was happily married—at least as happily as a married man can be. But . . .

Till one night when he happened to meet his friend, Panga. Over the inevitable beer. 'There's something missing in life, Panga, and I can't quite place it.'

Panga took a deep swig from his mug, placed it on the table with a flourish and spoke, 'Ranga boss, how long will you work for someone else? Isn't it time you branched out on your own?'

There were more discussions after that, but that one remark had set Ranga thinking. Even after reaching home, the thought kept nagging away. He couldn't sleep that night. And by the next morning, his decision was made. He was going to quit his job and start off on his own. The only question was, 'Doing what?'

Strangely enough, the answer was not far to seek. Both the organizations that Ranga had worked with had had a common problem: Feedback and suggestions from junior employees almost never reached the top. Being youngsters, these juniors had a kind of freshness in their thinking. Even when they complained, they usually had a solution which the seniors had not thought of. Both organizations he had worked for prided themselves on the fact that they were employee-driven (of course, the employees did not think so, but we'll let that pass). The issue was that most employees were too scared of giving feedback, especially when it concerned one of the pet schemes of the CEO or the other directors. The obvious solution was to create a suggestion box. However, this had one major disadvantage. The management had no way of finding out how many people agreed with each suggestion. Further, each suggestion could possibly lead to further thinking and therefore add-on suggestions from other employees. This would require a discussion thread, which was potentially invaluable. But with a suggestion box, there was no way to start a discussion thread.

Ranga realized that this was a very real problem faced by most organizations. And so he created a SaaS-based solution, BoloBolo. With a very professional-looking interface, aiming to capture feedback and other suggestions from employees. The software could accept feedback both from named employees as well as those who wanted to remain anonymous. Interestingly, all suggestions—whether anonymous or otherwise—permitted employees to vote. So, if someone agreed with a particular suggestion, she could vote for it and that suggestion would then get a score of two, and so on. The management would then be able to focus on those suggestions that had the support of a large enough number of employees, rather than being swamped with thousands of suggestions. In its next avatar, BoloBolo would also permit the option of starting a discussion thread. Once again, the management could focus on those suggestions that had spawned the largest thread. As I've already mentioned, the business would work in SaaS mode, with the client paying per user licence per month.

Ranga tried out a pilot in a couple of large organizations. Unpaid, of course. And it seemed to work fine in both cases. The management was happy, and was considering deploying the solution on a bigger scale. Ranga was satisfied, and believed that the time had now come for growth. Which meant raising funds, of course. For sales, for support, and for further development of the website. And who did Ranga go to? Angels, of course. So, let's go straight to the angel investor meet.

After listening to lots of bright, pink-faced youngsters fresh from college, the angels around the table found Ranga to be a refreshing change. Here was a person with experience. Someone who had seen the world and knew how to make things work. And, of course, he was solving a real problem. All of them had faced similar situations in their respective organizations, and they realized that this was a problem worth tackling. In simple terms, 'Idea *mein dum hai* (There is substance in the idea)' was the refrain across the table. The size of the market was large— all medium to large organizations were potential targets. And the solution was scalable—quite naturally, because it was completely online. No manual involvement at all. The angels also liked the single-minded focus of the entrepreneur—one problem, one solution, rather than trying out multiple things in the hope that something would work. And best of all, the founder. Experienced, mature, a DREAM Founder, if ever there was one. It seemed to be a good option.

But wait. There was something else. Something that one of the angels raised. 'What's your entry barrier?' he asked.

Ranga had anticipated this question. 'Over time, our brand will be an entry barrier. We also plan to bring in more and more enhancements, which will add value.'

'I don't agree,' said the angel. 'Your solution is actually fairly simple to program. Anyone else could easily copy it. In fact, the client organization itself could engage a programmer to create it. So why would they keep paying you every month?' Saying which the angel looked around proudly, expecting applause.

The applause did not come, but his comment had set the other angels thinking. Most of them concurred. This was not a particularly complex piece of software, and anyone could create it within a short period. The fact that the client organization itself could do it was a major risk. And with this, the angels started wavering.

Ranga used all his selling skills to convince the angels in the room, but they refused to be convinced. The risk was just too high. There wasn't even any revenue yet. One of them put it very well, 'Once you have the next version with appropriate enhancements, we can take a look again. But at this point, it's just too easy to copy.'

And with that, there was a collective nodding of wise heads across the table. This was not the right venture for their hard-earned money. At least, not yet. And that was that. Ranga had to be content with coffee after the meeting. Funding was nowhere on the horizon.

However, there is more to the story, so please read on. Over coffee, a somewhat morose Ranga was approached by our very own bearded professor (who else?). 'Don't be disheartened, young man,' the professor began, 'you have a good idea. The only thing is that you need to build your product further, so that it becomes tough to replicate in a hurry.'

'And there's something more. Entry barriers are not static. They simply give you some time before the other guy catches up. Once he's at par with you, there is effectively no barrier, isn't it? Therefore, you need to keep building your product continuously, in order to retain the entry barrier. Perhaps add some analytics. Maybe machine learning. What you add is your call. But once you've done that, and once you've got some traction, do get back to us. We would be interested.'

Ranga smiled. The morosity was gone (by the way, I'm fairly certain there is no such word in the English language, but it sounds so appropriate, doesn't it?). And with that, the two of them clinked their cups of coffee and said in one voice, 'Cheers!'

21

Getting Rural Artisans Online

Sattu (short for Satish) was a young graduate with a vision. No, a dream. He had read my book, and like all the successful entrepreneurs in it, he dreamt big. Real big. He lived in a cute little town called Solan in Himachal Pradesh, and his family came from a nearby village called Oachghat. Incidentally, as a youngster I have also lived in Solan, and my father had a farm in Oachghat, so I know the area very well. In his childhood, Satish would roam around Oachghat as well as the nearby villages such as Kalaghat, Padhan and Narag (as you can see, I do know that area—I am not fibbing). And he would watch the local people in action. As you can expect, most of them were into farming, but some of them, including the womenfolk, were artisans. They would make interesting kinds of pottery, handicrafts, toys, curios and so on. Real good stuff—even I've seen it. But they had no way to market it. That was the problem.

And that's where Sattu's dream took shape This young man wanted to create an online platform where he would market these local products. The customers would be individuals who wanted these items, as well as organizations that would use them as gifts for their clients. Thereby the artisans would have an outlet for their products, and Sattu would have a roaring business. A win-win for both, as you can see.

So Sattu built an online platform called GaonKiCheez, which was integrated with a payment gateway. And some revenues did start flowing in. But growth was not really picking up. He was able to get orders, but fulfilling them was an issue. Sattu racked his brains. And then racked them again. And again. But he wasn't able to solve the problem. Finally, he decided to get advice from someone he knew. And that's how he ended up sitting across the table with his mentor at Sirjees, the well-known halwai in Solan.

Who?

The bearded professor, of course.

The conversation began over yummy plates of chhole bhature. 'Sattu, you are doing good work,' said the professor. At which, of course, Sattu beamed and took a fresh bite of his bhatura. 'But you must realize that your current business model has a problem—scalability.'

'That's not a problem,' replied Sattu, as he chewed the somewhat leathery bhatura. 'I already have access to artisans in ten villages in Himachal and I plan to spread to other states like Rajasthan and Uttar Pradesh, which are well known for their highly skilled artisans. My target is to reach a hundred villages and increase my revenues tenfold.'

The professor was patient. 'Let me explain, Sattu. Scalability does not only mean growth. It means rapid growth. I accept the fact that over time you will be able to grow to, perhaps, a hundred villages. But here's the problem—each artisan will have a limited capacity for production, wouldn't she? For example, if someone is making pottery, she might be able to make, say, twenty pieces in a week. Or even fifty, provided she employs more people. That's a very small number. These ladies are not setting up large units, unlike GO DESi, which you've seen in chapter 18. They are working from home. So, the total production capacity of a village will always remain low. Which is why you will need to add a huge number of villages to get significant revenues. And that will take time. Lots of time.'

But there was still more, as the professor continued. 'The other issue with your business model is that it has no entry barrier. There are lots of people in this space. What is different about your business?'

'Sir, we will build up a brand. That will be our entry barrier.'

But the professor was persistent. Very patient, but persistent. 'No, my friend, brands take time to build. You need lots of happy customers, who keep coming back to you and refer you to their friends and colleagues. Brands are not built just because you have named your company—they are built in the minds of your customers. And that's one more reason to scale up rapidly—so you get a lot of happy customers, fast'.

'By the way, there is a way to make your business more scalable.'

At this, Sattu was all agog. In his excitement, even his rhythmic chewing had stopped. 'Please tell me how.'

'Sattu, I know that your thinking is very flexible. Use that flexibility and pivot your operational model. Let me explain. Suppose you were to appoint agents—people who manage a cluster of villages. For instance, you could have one agent in Solan district, who would cover that part of Himachal, another in Kullu, and another in Nahan. And if you wanted to go beyond Himachal to other states, perhaps one each in Jaipur, Udaipur, Jodhpur and Kota. These agents would locate potential artisans in the villages around them and put them up to you. Of course, the ultimate decision will be yours. But all the manual work of running around and identifying artisans is theirs. Not only that, once you have approved an artisan, the agent would pick up products from her and transport them to your warehouse. Again, all this manual work is his, for which he gets a commission. But the platform is yours, the customers are yours, and the brand is yours. And because you have delegated most of the human intervention to your agents, guess what? You've become more scalable!'

Of course, you can imagine Sattu's reaction. Delighted is not the word, as the chewing began in full force once again. 'Thank you, sir. That's a wonderful idea. I'll put this into action right away and get back to you once it is implemented.'

And so, the meeting ended, with a plate of rasmalai for each of them. Just to celebrate, you see? And yes, Sattu is now changing his operational model based on what his mentor had told him. He is in the process of appointing agents.

Hopefully, he will have a more scalable business now . . .

22

The Crowded, Crowded Food Delivery Space

This is a story about a young man who we will refer to by his nickname, AK47. As you might imagine, his initials were AK, and his friends called him AK47, so that's what we'll call him. Period.

AK47 lived in the small town of Chopal, and had always wanted to be an entrepreneur. He realized that people in small towns were keen on ordering food from restaurants and getting it delivered to their homes. He also felt that this was a huge, growing opportunity, not just in his hometown of Chopal, but also in many other small towns such as Gaipur, Sindore, Phansi and the like. Yes, it was a crowded space. In fact, both the giants Zomato and Swiggy were present in Chopal, but he was confident he could do a better job and charge less as well. And so, with the mandatory breaking of a coconut and the distribution of laddoos, AK Foods was born.

However, I'm sure you can imagine what happened next. Zomato and Swiggy were in no mood to give in to this upstart. In any case, they were known, trusted brands. And there was another problem. Many of the restaurants were competitors as well. They (the restaurants) clearly told customers that they (the restaurants) were happy to take on home deliveries themselves, and that they (the restaurants) would not charge extra, unlike them (AK Foods), and that their (the restaurants') service would be far better than theirs (AK Foods), so it made no sense to go to them (AK Foods), and instead the customer should order directly from them (the restaurants).

AK47 tried all the tricks in the trade and even reduced his delivery charges to near zero, but business simply refused to pick up. Utterly dejected, he was planning to shut down his business and perhaps take up a government job, when he happened to come to Delhi for a family wedding. And there he happened to meet our very own angel investor and mentor—the bearded professor. The professor invited AK47 to his favourite bar, and the two of them began their discussions over a beer (for the professor) and lassi (for AK47. You see, his parents had not let him pick up bad habits such as drinking alcohol. Incidentally, the bartender had a tough time organizing lassi, but finally managed, though there were a few sniggers among the staff).

'AK', the professor began, 'You are, of course, aware of the PERSISTENT business model, aren't you?'

'Yes sir,' said AK47, taking a sip of his tasteless lassi.

'So, you are aware that you should avoid getting into a crowded market. And food delivery is a hugely crowded market. Not only do you have the big guns—Zomato and Swiggy—but you also have local players. Even restaurant owners have got into the act.'

Another sip of lassi. 'Yes sir,' said the glum young man.

'So, what does the PERSISTENT model ask you to do? Identify a subset of this market, called a niche, which is not crowded. And, at the same time, is large enough. Right?

'Now look carefully around you. The town you live in—Chopal—has a lot of factories on the outskirts. There is CHEL, Prasim, JALCO, MAIL and several others. Each factory has a campus where all the employees live. And they have very few restaurants within or even close to the campus. Therefore, these employees have almost no options for ordering in. Does that give you an idea?'

'But sir, these industrial campuses are very far away from the main town, where we have the restaurants. CHEL is the closest, and that itself is some twenty-five kilometres away. I couldn't possibly deliver food to them and still make money.'

But the professor had other ideas. 'Young man, I want you to think. Do you really need to deliver food all day long? Suppose you tell the customers on campus that you will only deliver lunch, say between 1 p.m. and 2 p.m. either at their office or home. And dinner, between 8 p.m. and 9 p.m. That's it—just an hour each for lunch and dinner. Right now, people in the campus get no deliveries at all. Wouldn't they be delighted to get food from their favourite restaurant in Chopal? Even if it is within that one hour?'

Having got the young lassi-drinker to think, the professor then dropped his bombshell, 'And now, my friend, how would you make these deliveries? Would you send a delivery boy on his two-wheeler, carrying perhaps two or three orders out?'

By now, AK47 had got into the mood, 'Of course not, sir. I would send a three-wheeler carrying all the orders to be delivered to the entire campus. One three-wheeler for CHEL at lunchtime, and one at dinner time. Similarly, one three-wheeler for Prasim, one for JALCO, and so on. And therefore, my cost of delivery becomes very low, since one trip takes care of so many orders.' And AK47 actually started smiling as he ordered another lassi, to the chagrin of the bartender.

The professor smiled at AK47, as a hen might smile at its favourite chick. 'As you have rightly said, one reason why this will work is that you would have optimized your logistics—bunching up deliveries together! In other words, you have taken care of operations—the 'O' in our BOMB framework.'

By now, of course, AK47 was getting more and more excited. But the professor hadn't finished yet, 'Hang on. There is more. How do you take care of marketing to customers on these campuses?'

Of course, our young man was thinking. 'Why don't I contact the HR, or even the admin in-charge of the CHEL campus? He would probably be very happy, because it's a major benefit for his employees. I could request him to send a mail to all the employees asking them to download my app. So, I don't even need to spend on marketing. Wow, isn't this great?'

'Exactly. And this is what we call B2B2C marketing. Where your customer is the 'C', or consumer, but you go through his employer (the business, or 'B'). One of the most low-cost methods of marketing in use. So, you've taken care of low-cost operations as well as low-cost marketing. Great, isn't it?'

By now, of course, our young man was ecstatic. 'Sir, this sounds just perfect. I'll try it out immediately.'

And now, a question for you, dear reader. Would this concept work? Well, at the time of writing this book, AK47 was trying it out. You see, as a founder, you've got to have a flexible attitude. Keep trying out various options. Keep pivoting till things work out. Don't give up. Your business needs to be PERSISTENT, but you also need to be persevering, don't you?

Finally, I must tell you what happened at the end of the meeting. A charged-up AK47 went over to the bartender, 'Boss, enough lassi. I'll have a beer now!'

23

The Air Purifier That Didn't Take Off

Engi Kumar looked at the people coughing around him. 'Pollution level too high,' said one. 'Must get away to a less polluted place to survive,' said another. A third could not speak and had to get up for a glass of water. Now, Engi lived in Delhi and had been seeing the steadily deteriorating levels of pollution in the city. And it wasn't only Delhi. It was Mumbai, Bangalore, Chennai, Kolkata, and just about every other city in India. And there just didn't seem to be a solution.

That evening when Engi reached home, he was depressed. No, that's not correct. He was terribly depressed. Anyhow, he shut himself up in his bedroom, switched on the fancy, expensive air purifier he had bought a year ago, and settled down for the evening.

But he was thinking, 'In today's cities, a purifier has almost become a necessity. But most brands are expensive. Is it possible to have a lower cost product?'

Engi was unusually thoughtful over dinner. Even as he watched India defeat Australia in a T20 cricket match, his mind was elsewhere. That night he had a nightmare. He dreamt that he was with friends who were finding it difficult to breathe. He kept trying to give them his purifier and they were desperately reaching out for it, but were not able to grab it. This continued for several minutes, till at last he woke up with a start. It was still night, but he couldn't sleep any more. So, he made himself a stiff peg of you-know-what, and settled down to think.

Now, you might have guessed that Engi was an engineer, and a good one at that. He had cleared his BTech exam with a third division, but it was a very high third division. In fact, it was almost certain that he was the topper among all the third divisioners in his class. Of course, he was mighty proud of it. And as the liberal doses of alcohol warmed his insides in the cold Delhi winter, an idea began to take shape in his mind. He had to find a solution to the problem. Yes, that was it. God had sent him down to earth with a mission. To create a low-cost air purifier and make it available to the world. That was his dream.

Completely charged up by now, Engi took one last peg of his favourite drink—the stiffest one so far—and got into action. The next few weeks saw all his engineering know-how put into practice. Especially the subjects where he had got a comp (if you don't understand that term, a comp in a subject means that you have failed the exam and must repeat it. As if you didn't know). He spent some time studying existing purifiers, and figuring out how to make something that was more affordable. And finally one day, he had done it. Yes sir, he had made a truly affordable purifier. He went over to a friend who ran a small manufacturing unit. Between them they realized that the cost of such a purifier to the customer would be roughly half the cost of existing products.

Absolutely elated by now, Engi and his friend spent the rest of the evening drinking themselves silly (please don't get the wrong impression, they were not alcoholics. It was just to celebrate, you see). And after a day's break, because of the inevitable hangover when nothing could be done, they started work on the project as co-founders. Starting, of course, with patenting their solution!

Now, I don't want to bore you with details of how this purifier would work, and how it was different from the others. In any case, I didn't understand the functioning either, so I cannot explain it to you. But it did work. Anyhow, a few months later, they formally launched their purifier, which they had branded 'Saaf Hawa' (or Pure Air). They decided to sell it on Amazon and Flipkart. In addition, they tied up with a few dealers in Delhi for offline sales. And then, of course, they sat back and waited for the sales to roar!

Unfortunately, there was no roar. Not even a whimper. Yes, a few brave souls did buy their product, but these were few and far between. Completely confused and dejected by now, Engi decided to spend time with a couple of his dealers and listen to what their customers had to say. (By the way, this is extremely important. The best person to tell you what he thinks of your product is your customer. Even more so, the customer who considered buying it but finally didn't. Remember Sanjeev Bikhchandani's advice—get close to the customer?) Now, by sheer coincidence, I also happened to be at that particular dealership at that time, so I was able to listen to Engi's conversation with one customer who wanted to buy a purifier. The conversation was in Hindi, but to save paper, I'll give you the English version directly. This is how it went:

Dealer: 'Sir, this is a great new product, Saaf Hawa. Very effective and just half the price of the bigger brands such as Philips and Daikin.'

Customer (unimpressed): 'No, do you have something from Philips or Honeywell?'

As you can imagine, the conversation continued around Philips and Honeywell and Daikin. But no Saaf Hawa. At the end of which, the customer bought one of those brands, although he cribbed and cribbed about the high price. When this customer was leaving the shop, Engi went up to him, 'Sir, if you don't mind, I'm doing a survey. Why didn't you consider Saaf Hawa, even though it was priced so much lower?'

The customer looked at Engi as if he were a congenital idiot. But he was willing to talk, in fact, very willing. And, of course, he didn't know that this was Engi's own product. 'Young man, there are two reasons why I wouldn't buy this product. First of all, it's a local brand. In fact, it's unbranded (remember our discussion on brands in chapter 15?).' At which, of course, Engi winced as if he had been punched in the stomach. But that's irrelevant to this story, so let's carry on with what the customer said. 'You see, if I were to buy, say, an unbranded room cooler, I know it is working effectively because it is actually cooling the room. I can feel the temperature coming down. But in a purifier, I have absolutely no idea. It might be working, or it might not.'

'But sir,' interrupted Engi, 'there is a display which tells you the level of particulate impurities in the air. That will tell you whether or not it is working.'

'Again, unbranded! How do I know that's the right figure? The only way to ensure that this kind of product is working is to buy a solid, trusted brand.'

Spirits sinking, Engi realized that the customer was right. For a product where you really couldn't figure out whether it was working effectively, brand and trust were supremely important. As the customer turned to leave, Engi suddenly remembered something, 'Sir, you mentioned two reasons. What is the second one?'

'Ah yes, of course. Maintenance. If for some reason it stops functioning—perhaps the blower doesn't work, or it doesn't switch on at all—who will repair it? This is not the kind of product where you'll have mechanics at every street corner who can repair it. And therefore, I'll need to get back to the company—what's their name—Saaf Hawa. But do they have enough service centres? Will they send a person home? I have no idea. And therefore, I would rather go with one of the large, trusted brands, even if I have to spend more. Because I know that maintenance will be taken care of.'

And as this gentleman walked out, he had a last word of advice for poor Engi, 'Young man, if you are planning to buy a purifier, I would strongly suggest Philips or Honeywell. Or even Daikin.'

As you can imagine, Engi was stumped. By the way, he met many customers that day and the feedback was more or less the same. Completely dejected by now, he trudged back home to make himself—you guessed it—the stiffest drink of the year.

Dear reader, I don't need to explain anything here, do I? Going back to our good, old PERSISTENT model, Engi might have had a great product, but did he really have an earnings model? In other words, would the customer pay for it? Wouldn't he rather buy a more expensive, but trusted brand? And then, of course, we have our BOMB approach as well, where Engi got stuck in marketing, simply because he didn't have a trusted brand. And also in operations, because he needed a large customer support network to give his customers confidence.

Incidentally, there are many other situations where a trusted brand is the only way to verify whether or not the product is genuine. Take, for instance, organic food: How do you know whether the food is genuinely organic? Will you do exhaustive tests to check for the presence of harmful pesticides or chemical fertilizers? Of course not! Or take vegan products—how do you know that milk has not been added surreptitiously to the products? You see? There are lots of situations where the customer cannot figure out the genuineness of a product. And that's where a trusted brand becomes so critical!

And now for the big question. Engi had developed a great product. Functional, as well as far more affordable than anything else in the market. It was also patented. But it wasn't selling. Could he have done something different?

Of course, he could! Remember, we had spoken about strategic investors in chapter 17? What if these founders had approached such an investor—let's say a well-known brand in the consumer appliances space such as Bajaj, Usha or Symphony, and asked one of them to make a strategic investment in their start-up? These guys had applied for a patent, so that was not an issue anyway. Our young friends could do the manufacturing, and the strategic investor could sell it under its brand as well as take care of maintenance. With a strong brand involved, trust would not be an issue. And with its countrywide reach, neither sales nor maintenance would be a problem. A win-win for both companies, as you can see.

Would this work? Well, I don't know, but it is definitely worth trying. And that's what founders need to do, isn't it? Keep trying out options.

But will Engi? Ah, I don't know. I've told him to, and he liked the idea. Maybe he's waiting for his next stiff drink.

Let's Meet Meena Ganesh, founder, chairperson and MD, Portea Medical

Of course you've heard of Meena Ganesh. The hugely successful founder, chairperson and managing director of Portea Medical—the market leader in anything to do with healthcare services at home. But what you don't know (and I'm not surprised you don't) is that Meena and I were colleagues at NIIT many years ago. And we had a wonderful time working on projects together. Which is why, when I started writing this book and wanted to interview highly successful founders in the Indian start-up space, she was one of the first people I thought of.

Meena was more than happy to share her views. By the way, as you can imagine, she is a very busy person. So, I got my interview when she was on a vacation with her family in Mexico (sorry Meena, for messing up your holiday). Anyhow, this is what she had to say:

The starting point for any successful founder (or a DREAM Founder, as Dhruv puts it), is a clear vision or dream of what you want to do. And it cannot be a tiny, microscopic dream. It has to be big. Something that disrupts the market. You must push the limits, and dream of something that has perhaps not even been tried before. Of course, you must be passionate about this vision. Because that will give you the will and the energy to pursue it, even when you have roadblocks such as Covid, along the way.

The other crucial bit is that you must be flexible. An arrogant attitude, where you believe you cannot be wrong, can kill the business. Your way may not be the only way to run the business. Be prepared to accept the fact that you could be wrong, and be willing to look at alternatives. Pivot the business model if necessary. Most successful start-up founders are extremely flexible in their approach. If they find that something is not working, they are more than willing to relook at the business model. To adapt to changes in the market, or the environment, or the emergence of competition, or even changes in government policy.

And now for execution. Having a dream is not enough. You must have the ability to get into execution mode. In this context, let me revisit the issue of arrogance. Many founders are under the mistaken impression that they can do everything. No way. For two reasons: First of all, you have only twenty-four hours a day, and there is a limit to what you can do as an individual. And secondly, different kinds of skills are required for running a business. You need skills in marketing, product development, programming, operations, accounts . . . The list goes on. Tell me truthfully, do you have the necessary skills to do all these? Of course not. You need multiple people in your team. People who bring different skills to the table. And therefore, team building is another key priority for any founder. Build your team. Give up some control—don't breathe down the necks of your employees all the time. Give them a chance to make mistakes. That's the only way these guys will learn and develop. And that's the only way you can build your team.

Finally, I do hope this helps all the young founders reading this book. All the very best to each one of you!

Great advice. Thank you so, so much, Meena. And I promise not to mess up your next family vacation!

Section V

Making Opportunities out of Crises

24

Khow Suey at Auntie Fung's

And now for the real big test of DREAM Founders—namely, how they react to a crisis. All of you are aware of the crisis we had in 2020—the Covid pandemic. Perhaps the biggest in a hundred years. Cities were in lockdown for months—and when they did attempt to surface, they were forced into lockdown again. Quite naturally, most businesses were hit hard, and many simply folded up. Now, in these overwhelmingly tough times, you had two kinds of founders. The first kind had a simple reaction, '*Mar gaya. Kuchh nahin kar sakta hoon* (in Hindi)'; or '*Morey gailo. Kichhu, korte pari na* (in chaste Bengali)'; or if you prefer, 'I'm dead. Can't do anything right now (in English, of course).' This kind alternated between cursing the virus and watching Netflix. But there were a few who were made of sterner stuff. These were the founders who decided to fight it out. They were flexible and were willing to pivot their business in order to survive. In fact, the best of them actually MADE an OPPORTUNITY out of the CRISIS. Yes, my friend. A crisis is what truly separates the men from the boys—or the ladies from the girls!

Incidentally, start-ups have faced lots of other crises as well. For instance, as you have seen in chapter 3, Instamojo faced a crisis where their money ran out and funding was not available. And the founders grabbed the opportunity to make the business more efficient. Many start-ups, which used to get payments in cash, floundered during the demonetization drive of 2016. Some years earlier, during the global financial crisis, not just start-ups, but even large corporations went bankrupt. Yes, you could have crises of all kinds. But for the moment, let's talk about Covid. And the story of an interesting start-up called Auntie Fung's.

For a start, I have a question for you. How would you like to have a dish of khow suey? Don't know what that is? Okay, what about nasi goreng? No? Okay, mee goreng. Still no? All right, last attempt—what about pho? No again? Well, clearly you haven't really tried Asian cuisine. You see, khow suey is a delectable Burmese dish. Nasi goreng and mee goreng are popular dishes in Indonesia as well as Malaysia. And pho is a kind of staple food in Vietnam. All these are rather like chhole bhature in north India, or pav bhaji in Mumbai, or even idli sambhar in the South. They are local dishes, very popular in the geographies in which they are made and served. Trust me—I've tried all of them and they are yummy!

Now, I could go on and on about how tasty these dishes are, but that's a subject for another book. So, let's not waste any more time and pages, and talk about the DREAM Founders of this company. In this case, two young men—Subhradeep Bhowmik and Satrajit Das. Both old friends from their school days, and both MBAs. And what's even more important, both foodies—although when I met them, their respective figures did not bear this out. Till the year 2015, Subhradeep held a series of well-paying jobs in great companies—TCS, GE and Johnson & Johnson. But somewhere there was an itch. 'I must start something on my own. And it has to be in the area of food.' And one fine day, he quit his job and decided to become an entrepreneur. In the process roping in his friend Satrajit as a co-founder.

The obvious question was, within the food business, what? You see, if there is one business that you will find in every nook and corner of each city, each town and each village in our country, it is food outlets. Every second commercial establishment is a restaurant, a dhaba, an udupi, a halwai, a sweet shop, or simply a cart on the street selling gol gappas (which are called puchkas or paani pooris, depending on which part of the country you live in. Or even water balls, in case you happen to be silly enough to walk into a five-star hotel and order chaat of all things). Adding one more kind of food outlet to the crores that already existed would have been stupid, wouldn't it?

So, these guys thought and thought. And when they had finished, they thought some more. And slowly, ever so slowly, an idea began to take shape. You see, Subhradeep had travelled all over South-East Asia and had really liked the local street food there. Dishes such as nasi goreng and khow suey, which I had mentioned in the beginning of this story (don't tell me you've forgotten these names already!). Dishes from Vietnam, Malaysia, Indonesia, Myanmar and . . .

Yes, Chinese food was very common in India. To some extent, so was Japanese food. But Vietnamese food? Burmese food? Indonesian food? Pan-Asian food? No way. Well, that's not strictly correct. There were some fine-dining restaurants in India serving these delectable dishes, but these were beyond the reach of most Indian wallets. And that's where our young friends had a brainwave. Why not create a dhaba-like affordable restaurant for pan-Asian food? Or udupi-like, if you prefer? In fact, why not create a chain of these outlets? The more these guys thought about it, the more they warmed up to the idea. Yes, this was a major gap in the Indian market and needed to be plugged. And so, over the inevitable beer and clinking of mugs, the decision was made— they would launch a chain of affordable, dine-in restaurants for pan-Asian street food!

Having taken this momentous decision, the next step was to create an interesting sounding name. Now tell me, when you think of a great cook, who do you think of? Typically, some aunt in the neighbourhood, isn't it? To cash in on this thought, our friends decided to call it Auntie Fung's. Why Fung's? Well, it could easily have been Auntie Song's, Auntie Ming's, or even Auntie Pang's. But they finally plumped for Auntie Fung's. Incidentally, in case you ever want to create something along these lines, you are welcome to call it Uncle Mong's or anything else that you like— that's your prerogative!

And then of course, there was another decision point. Which cities? They would have loved to launch Auntie Fung's outlets all over the country, but that would have been too humongous a task. So, they had to restrict it to one, or at the most two cities. Which ones? Well, Subhradeep was based in Bangalore, so that is where they launched their first restaurant. And then waited for the response. And was it popular? Of course, it was. Chinese food was commonly available, but customers had never tried yummy Vietnamese, Indonesian or Burmese food. They lapped it up. So much so, that by January 2020, these young men had ramped up to seven outlets. Which included kiosks in malls across Bangalore— and, by now, Gurgaon as well. Things were all hunky-dory and our young friends started dreaming of how they would expand.

But of course, you know what happened next. March 2020 brought with it Covid, and with it, the countrywide lockdown. And for Auntie Fung's, it couldn't have been worse, because many of their outlets were in malls, which were completely shut. The only one that continued to function was their original outlet, which was not in a mall, and was therefore open for takeaways. That's it. Naturally, business almost came to a grinding halt. No dining in, no customers, and no pan-Asian food. Period.

Now, our young friends could easily have sat back and watched Netflix. Or even played video games twenty-three hours a day, waiting for the stupid virus to go away (they would still need to sleep for at least an hour, you see). And, of course, curse their luck in between games. But no. These founders were made of sterner stuff. Much sterner stuff. Of course, they also had just the right attitude—they were flexible. And, in one of their bright moments, they realized something interesting. Yes, restaurants were closed and people were forced to stay indoors. But they were still eating. More importantly, after the initial days of the lockdown, they were still ordering in, thanks to Zomato and Swiggy. And this is where the two young men sensed a glimmer of an opportunity. 'We have our recipes. We have chefs who are experts in this kind of cuisine. And we've built up a brand in these two cities. The fact that customers are ordering in from the one outlet of ours that is open is proof. The only thing that has changed is that dining-in is not permitted. So why don't we create cloud kitchens instead of dine-in restaurants? And use these to deliver our yummy khow suey and nasi goreng to customers through Zomato and Swiggy?'

By the way, you obviously know what cloud kitchens are. But for your friend who doesn't, here is a simple explanation: Cloud kitchens are kitchens that are set up only for food delivery, as against dine-in restaurants as well as kiosks, where the food is cooked and eaten on the spot. Restaurants and kiosks need to be located in places where customers would land up for an outing—places such as popular markets or even malls. And this is the key—these places are expensive. In addition, they need to be done up attractively. Once again, that's expensive! Cloud kitchens, on the other hand, have no such restrictions on their location. They could be located in low-cost areas. And no fancy interiors are required—simply because no customer would ever come there. The only people who would come there are the chefs and, of course, the delivery boys from Zomato or Swiggy. And that's the fundamental advantage of building cloud kitchens—very low cost of operations.

Of course, it took our founders a few months to pivot from the dine-in model to the cloud kitchen model. After all, they had to locate spaces for their cloud kitchens, sign rental agreements, and ultimately set them up. In addition, given the fact that these were Covid times, clear safety protocols needed to be established. But once that was done, Auntie Fung's launched their cloud kitchens in Bangalore and Gurgaon.

And what do you think happened? Will you believe me if I tell you? Yes sir, within a year of the initial lockdown, their revenues were more than twice what they had been during the pre-Covid days. And they also raised a round of angel funding in the process. That's right, these guys had not only survived, but grown during Covid. Even through the second wave!

But that's not the end of the story. There are a couple of other things that these young men did, which you and I can learn from. Remember the PERFECT ATTITUDE I had discussed in chapter 4? Where I had spoken about being customer-oriented? Well, what do you think customers' thinking was during and after the lockdown? Safety, safety, safety! Customers needed to trust anyone that they were ordering from. And to let you know what Auntie Fung's did, let's hear out Subhradeep:

It was extremely important to build trust in the minds of consumers, especially during Covid times. And we realized that the best way to do this was to permit them to connect directly with us founders. So, in each packet of food that we delivered, we included an email ID. And no, not the usual 'customer care' email ID. The email ID was founders@auntiefungs.com. If a customer had an issue or a question, he or she could connect directly with one of us founders, and not a junior person from a call centre. By the way, we did get lots of emails, which we responded to. And I believe this simple act of ours went a long way in building the kind of trust that the consumer needed to have in our brand.

But there is more. Yes, these guys were building trust in their customers. But what about their team? When the lockdown was imposed, lakhs of people lost their jobs. And what happened at Auntie Fung's? Believe it or not, no one lost his job. I repeat, *no one lost his job*. Yes, for some time after the lockdown, salaries had to be reduced because revenues were badly hit. However, our founders were transparent about their revenues, and as the revenues grew, salaries started getting back to pre-Covid days.

Now there is still more, so please keep reading. You may not be aware that employees in a restaurant are usually provided food and accommodation as part of their package. Not five-star accommodation, but something like a hostel. And Auntie Fung's continued to provide this. In other words, while salaries were reduced, everyone in the team had a roof over his head and three square meals a day. Brilliant, wasn't it? Can you think of a better way to build trust in the team?

However, I am still not done, so let's hear out Subhradeep once again:

> We realized that we had some spare capacity in our cloud kitchens. And therefore, we decided to launch another brand, which we called Crazy Bao (in case you didn't know, a bao is something like a steamed burger, Chinese style). With the same chefs and the same cloud kitchens churning out these baos, so there was no additional fixed cost. Interestingly, we dished up baos such as butter chicken bao, chicken chettinad bao, and paneer makhani bao, in keeping with the requirements of Indian palates. Hindi-Chini bhai-bhai, you might say. Or perhaps Hindi-Chini bao-bao!

Dear reader, can you see how these founders had made an opportunity out of the crisis? They pivoted to food delivery through the cloud kitchen model. They successfully built trust in their customers as well as their team. And, of course, they launched another brand from within the same cloud kitchens. Can you possibly ask for more from DREAM Founders?

And with that, dear reader, let me leave you dreaming about khow suey, and nasi goreng and, of course, butter chicken bao. But don't forget to order these dishes.

From our very own Auntie Fung's, of course!

25

How Gadget Restore Became Grest

This is another story about two of my students from MDI, Shrey Sardana and Nitin Goyal. A few years back, these young men had started an interesting company called Gadget Restore, where they would repair smartphones. And since then, it has been a fascinating journey. Wouldn't you want to hear it? OK, here goes . . .

These two young men were fascinated by the rapid and continuous changes taking place in technology, particularly in the smartphone space. Now, I'm sure you are aware of what happens when a new phone is launched (if you're not, you are probably living in the past century). Young people—and even some older ones—simply have to buy it. Just imagine two young boys competing for the same girlfriend. The first one flaunts the latest iPhone, and the other one has a model that is more than a year old. Obsolete. Wouldn't you feel sorry for the poor, miserable second boy? Unfair competition, isn't it? And so, everyone simply rushes to buy the newer model the moment it is launched. In the process, trading in his old phone. The company that buys these old phones, repairs them and then sells them back in the used phone market. And this was the opportunity our founders grabbed. Because many of these companies used to ask Gadget Restore to repair these old phones, rather than do it themselves. A wonderful partnership, as you can imagine. And life carried on . . .

But not for long. In early 2020, the dreaded Covid virus hit the world, and India went into a lockdown. However, you are aware that these young men were DREAM Founders (obvious, isn't it? That's how they made it to this book). They were willing to be totally flexible with their business model. So they put on their thinking caps, picked up enormous glasses of lassi, and thought and thought. And when the lassi stopped working, they switched to beer. And thought some more. And more . . .

And suddenly, while gulping down their nth mug of beer, it hit them. Yes sir, they had a brainwave. (They're not sure which one of them had this brainwave. You see, after so much beer, you tend to forget such minor details. But it was clearly a brainwave.) Our young friends realized that Covid had forced schools and colleges to shut down. No physical classes. But—and this was the crucial but—education had to continue. And continue it did, in online mode.

Now, I'm sure you can guess the rest.

No? Okay, let me give you a hint. Every schoolgoing child needed access to a smartphone. Now can you guess?

Still no? Okay, let me give you an even bigger hint. While all children needed a smartphone, many of them came from low-income families. And therefore, they could not buy a new phone. On the other hand, many of them could afford second-hand ones. But there was a catch. Nitin put it very well, so let's hear him out:

We spent some time researching the market for phones. And we realized something very important: What was reliable was not affordable. And what was affordable was not reliable. The reliable phones were the new ones with a warranty from the manufacturer. But they were expensive. And the affordable ones were second-hand phones—typically bought from mom-and-pop stores. Usually in poor condition with no warranty at all. And that's the opportunity we grabbed. We decided to launch phones that were affordable as well as reliable!

You see, these two young men were already in the business of repairing phones. But now they decided to take it one step further and create refurbished ones. So, they bought second-hand phones from the market, many of which were not in working condition. And then they not only repaired them, but also did 'cosmetic surgery' on them to make them look like new phones. They then created their own B2C brand called Grest (which comes from Gadget RESTore) and sold these phones as refurbished phones under this brand. Not as new phones, you understand. Our founders believed in being completely ethical, so as to build trust among their customers. In other words, a Samsung phone was still sold as a Samsung phone, but under the refurbished brand, Grest. With Grest giving their customers a one-year warranty. Which meant that if something went wrong with the phone, well, Grest would support the customer. These founders were fully customer-oriented, as you can see.

Of course, you can imagine what happened. Lots of parents were desperate to get reliable, low-cost phones for their schoolgoing children. Now suddenly, they had a solution. Phones that worked well, looked like new phones and had a warranty. And, of course, they were much cheaper than the originals. As you can imagine, business boomed. The demand was huge because such refurbished phones, that too with a warranty, were simply not available in the market. And Grest happily satisfied this demand. Can you see how the founders had pivoted and made an opportunity out of the Covid crisis?

But that's not all. No sir, DREAM Founders are restless people. They do not sit back and relax. They are constantly looking for new opportunities. And our young friends realized that there was another opportunity waiting to be tapped. Let's hear Shrey on what happened:

We realized that Covid had brought with it another opportunity.
It is true that many students needed affordable smartphones.

But there were many who wanted affordable laptops. And with work-from-home becoming the norm, even working professionals were looking for affordable and reliable laptops. Having sensed this opportunity, we acquired a company which was into laptop repairs. Based on which, we launched our second product under the Grest brand—refurbished laptops.

At the time of writing this book, Grest phones and laptops were available in over twenty-five outlets across several locations, including Gurgaon and Jaipur, as well as several towns in Uttarakhand and Gujarat. In fact, given the strong demand, Grest has three exclusive stores. And most of these stores offer post-sales support as well. Today, Grest sells an average of over 500 devices a month. And that figure is only going up and up . . .

One last point. These founders have been profitable from the first year itself. Yes, even I did not believe it. And they are completely bootstrapped. Truly remarkable DREAM Founders, don't you think?

And now, in case you want to buy a Grest phone or a laptop, look no further. Just land up at one of the Grest outlets in Gurgaon. If you're lucky, you could also meet one of the founders. And believe me, you won't regret your purchase.

In fact, they will even treat you to lassi. Just tell them I sent you!

26

The Bright Sparks of PlanetSpark

We are now close to the end of this book. And I always like to end with a bang. Which is why I will now tell you one of my most dramatic stories—the story of PlanetSpark. This story has everything. It has DREAM Founders. The business itself is fully in keeping with the PERSISTENT model—although these guys probably haven't heard of the term (a situation that I must correct the next time I meet them over coffee). Most importantly, the founders have converted the Covid pandemic into a massive opportunity, and are today market leaders in their chosen space.

What do they do? Well, to find out, you'll have to read on . . .

I met the two young founders of PlanetSpark, Maneesh Dhooper and Kunal Malik, in the open-air canteen at MDI, Gurgaon. They had done their MBA from XLRI in Jamshedpur, which is where they had met each other (incidentally, that is one more reason why I wanted to talk about them. You see, I didn't want you to get the impression that I only wrote about my students from MDI. Kunal and Maneesh were from XLRI, and therefore they were definitely not my students. So, I hope that clears up any misunderstanding you might have had!).

Anyhow, to get back to my story, these two founders had spent a few years working with great organizations such as Hindustan Unilever and Novartis. But then they were hit by the inevitable.

Yes, you guessed right, it was the entrepreneurship bug. And that was the end of their jobs and the fat salaries they used to get at the end of each month. The two young men decided that enough was enough and they simply had to do something on their own. Period.

Interestingly, both friends were interested in children's education, so their dream was clear—it had to be something in this space. And of course, it had to be big. But what? They started exploring the space, and very soon they zoomed in on the huge market for tuition classes. As you are aware, Indian parents are extremely keen to spend on the education of their children. And one of the natural consequences has been the mushrooming of tuition classes—whether it is in tuition centres, or simply at the dining table in the home of the tutor. The founders realized that while the opportunity was huge, it was a highly unorganized space with quality and standardization suffering in many cases. Just imagine a young child sitting with her tutor in the tutor's house, with the tutor's maid in a heated argument with the milkman. Or the whistle of the pressure cooker blowing every few minutes. Or the tutor's phone ringing non-stop. Can you blame the poor kid for not being able to concentrate?

So far, there was no choice. But with Kunal and Maneesh entering the picture, finally there was a choice. Because now the child had PlanetSpark. What did these young men do? Very simple. They decided to launch high-quality, standardized, technology-enabled learning centres for children from classes two to eight. Why not beyond class eight? Too much competition— and the founders rightly wanted to target a market that was not crowded (remember our PERSISTENT framework?). They started by focusing on English and Maths and built a large amount of digital content as well as physical workbooks for these subjects. And then they had a brainwave. They decided to tie up with OYO Rooms, where OYO would let them have a room in some of their properties in residential areas. And this is where PlanetSpark launched their learning centres in 2017. Armed with laptops, lots of exciting digital content and of course, workbooks for each class and each subject. And all this under the watchful eye of a mentor, who would guide the students.

I've been to one of the centres, and believe me, I found it really impressive. And so did lots of parents and their schoolgoing children, because business boomed. When I met these founders, they already had fifty centres in the city of Gurgaon. And were well on their way to doubling or even tripling them. They had already raised a round of funding from FIITJEE—the well-known market leader in helping students prepare for entrance exams. And with the promise the business showed, the founders easily managed the second round of funding in 2019. A round in which FIITJEE participated once again, along with Lead Angels, Indian Angel Network and Hyderabad Angels. Yes sir, everything was just hunky-dory.

Well, not quite. Because then, Covid hit. With the strict lockdown that followed, these young men were forced to shut down all those wonderful learning centres. But, of course, that didn't deter them. Like many other founders of edtech companies, they realized that learning would continue to be a high priority for parents. But at least in the foreseeable future, it would be online. And therefore, Kunal and Maneesh made all their wonderful learning material available online. Even the mentors were accessible online and the learning centres continued—albeit in virtual mode.

But as you can imagine, they had a problem. A major problem. Online learning for children was a very, very crowded space. With the likes of Byju's, Toppr, Vedantu and all the other giants. To go back to our PERSISTENT model, the market size was huge, but it was extremely crowded. And these guys had to find a niche within this space that was large enough but not crowded. And that's when they got into experimentation mode. They tried extracurricular activities such as painting, music and dance. They even developed learning material around robotics. Kunal and Maneesh were both highly persevering young men and were willing to try out multiple options to find out what their customers wanted. They were truly customer-oriented. And so, the experimentation continued . . .

And that's when something clicked. Yes, it really did. You would remember that these guys were covering English as part of their curriculum. One of the things they covered there was English communication—both oral and written. Our young friends realized that this might be the large niche they were looking for. So, they revised the material they had and launched a new product—'Public Speaking and Creative Writing'. Once again with teachers as mentors. And this really clicked. Parents were very keen to give their children the confidence to face the world of tomorrow, and public speaking seemed to be just the thing. They simply lapped up the offering.

But that's not all. Since their offering was no longer curriculum linked, it was not limited to any country. Our founders realized this and decided to go global. To markets such as the USA and the Middle East. In these countries, the revenue per child would be much higher than it was in India, but the costs would be the same since the mentors were from India. In other words, revenues increased dramatically and so did the margins. Smart, wasn't it?

Today, PlanetSpark is a global player, helping children across the world develop their presentation and creative writing skills in English. Now, can you see how our founders had truly made an opportunity out of the crisis? They had to shut down their earlier business because of Covid, but were able to pivot to a more focused business, which is booming today.

Of course, as DREAM Founders, they ticked all the other boxes as well. Let's hear out Maneesh on how they built the right team:

> Right from the beginning, we were very careful about the people we recruited. We wouldn't just take on people for whom it was just another job. It had to be people who wanted to do what we were doing. They had to share in our dream. For instance, we would check if they had researched what we were doing. If not, they were probably not the right guys anyway. So, our interviews were long and searching.
>
> And having taken people on, we spent a lot of time with them initially, to make them comfortable. Once that was done, we gave them a lot of freedom. No micro-management—although our organization structure and reporting has always been strong. In fact, some of our guys have told me that they never expected to get a chance to do big things almost independently. And that too, at such an early stage. That's why people stayed with us. And that's one major reason for our success.

But I haven't finished with the PlanetSpark story yet. There are two more critical things these guys did as part of their execution strategy. First of all, marketing. Yes, they spent on semi-fixed marketing, which was largely digital. But they focused very strongly on SEO, or search engine optimization. Which, as you are aware, is almost zero-cost marketing. In fact, if you were to do a Google search on 'public speaking for children', PlanetSpark would probably come out on top. Just try it out!

The other interesting thing they did was to use their teachers as partners. Remember, each teacher would have her own students anyway, quite apart from the students she taught through PlanetSpark. Each teacher would be given discount coupons, which she could share with her existing students. And many of these students signed up for PlanetSpark's courses. Pure variable cost marketing. Smart, wasn't it?

The rest, as they say, is history. PlanetSpark has been growing rapidly, and is today a clear market leader in its chosen space in India. The founders have raised a total of four rounds of funding so far. And can you guess how the valuation has grown? Believe it or not, the latest funding has been raised at a valuation of—hold your breath—one hundred and fifty times what they had got in the first round. And this in just three and a half years. Can you imagine anything more spectacular?

And with that, we must say goodbye to Kunal and Maneesh. As these true DREAM Founders continue their wonderful journey towards making great public speakers out of children.

And, of course, their rapid journey towards becoming a unicorn.

27

When Pink Slips Are Needed

And now for the very last story. Paisadubao.com was in trouble. In case you are not aware, this was an extremely interesting start-up in the space of wealth management. Now, I can anticipate your next question, 'What the hell is wealth management?' Well, a wealth manager is someone who helps people manage their money, their investments, their loans, their insurance, etc. In short, their entire finances. As the term implies, wealth managers are used by wealthy people who are keen to become even more wealthy—as if they needed to!

So, Paisadubao was in the business of wealth management. But no, not for wealthy people. Not for Ratan Tata or Narayana Murthy or even the Birla family. Come on, don't be silly. These people have enough wealth managers to take care of their money and invest it. They don't need Paisadubao.com. So, who needs it? The common man of course—or the aam aadmi, if you prefer. People like you and me, who cannot afford the services of expensive wealth managers. Yes, Paisadubao became a kind of affordable, app-based wealth manager for people like us. And, of course, with the great brand name, Paisadubao, they were certain to go places.

The founder of the company was Motubhai Founderbhai, a distant cousin of Haribhai Founderbhai, or Harry, who you've already met in chapter 9. Motu had put his own savings into the company. In addition, he had begged and borrowed from his family and friends (as far as I am aware, he did not steal). And in the process, he managed to put together a war chest of Rs 50 lakh, with which he developed a basic app and started the marketing process. He did manage to onboard a few customers, but for some strange reason, growth came to a standstill after that. And of course, the cash burn refused to come down. Which meant that the bank balance came down relentlessly, and in fact, showed no signs of any deceleration. Why did this happen? I don't really know. Perhaps the concept was taking time to pick up. Or maybe there were too many other players trying the same thing. Whatever the reason, Motu was getting into a precarious situation. Perhaps a full-blown crisis. And he realized he had to cut costs. In fact, cut them dramatically.

But which ones? There were many minor items, but he quickly focused on the two big ones, namely marketing and salaries. Now obviously, he couldn't cut marketing costs—in fact he should have probably increased the spend on marketing, given that he desperately needed revenues. And that meant—that's right, you've guessed it—he needed to reduce his salary bill. Which meant that some people had to go.

The next couple of days were among the toughest our friend Motu had ever faced. He had built this team. He had nurtured each member. He had treated each person like a family member, and now he would have to ask some of them to leave. Hand out pink slips, if you are aware of the term. It was so unfair . . .

However, he realized that if he kept everyone on, the company would probably shut shop and therefore, everyone would be out of a job. And so, he got down to the unpleasant task of figuring out who to let go. Actually it wasn't too difficult. Marketing was critical, and therefore the two marketing guys had to stay. Customer support was equally important, to hang on to the existing customers. That left his team of five programmers, including one team lead. Motu realized that the team lead was indispensable. Plus, he needed to retain one more programmer—after all, maintenance issues and tweaking could come up at any stage. But developing the next version of the product could be delayed, and therefore, three programmers were—he hated the term—dispensable.

The next day, he called in these programmers one by one. And the conversation with each of them was the same. 'Unfortunately, we are facing tough times right now. And we need to cut manpower costs to survive.' Of course, you can imagine the reaction of the poor guys across the table as they sat quietly, listening to this thunderbolt. But just hear out what Motu said next. 'You have been a great asset for our company. And I cannot just ask you to leave. So, I've spoken to three friends of mine. All of them run start-ups and they are all doing well. I also checked with them—they all need programmers with your kind of background. They are all willing to meet you and see if they can absorb you into their company. Till then, you will remain on our rolls.'

You can imagine the reaction. On the one hand, each of these young programmers realized that he had lost his job. On the other hand, here was the boss actively helping him to find another job. This was unheard of, and the respect they had for Motu simply doubled in that one simple meeting.

Of course, you know what happened next (remember this is not a tragedy—maybe I'll write that kind of book later). All three youngsters were able to land jobs in the start-ups that Motu had referred them to. And when that happened, there was a party in the Paisadubao office. Because no one was losing his job. These youngsters were simply moving from one job to another. If anything, the bonding in Paisadubao's team became even stronger.

But my story is not over yet. A year later, revenues in Paisadubao picked up, and Motu went into recruitment mode again. And guess what? He was deluged with applications. Word of mouth had spread, and Paisadubao was among the most trusted employers around.

Yes, my friend, Motubhai had truly made an opportunity out of the crisis he faced. He had used the crisis to build trust in the company. And to bind the team even closer together.

But isn't that what DREAM Founders are all about?

Let's Meet Sushanto Mitra, founder and CEO, Lead Angels

Dear reader, you've now met some of the best-known founders in the business. Founders such as Deep Kalra of MakeMyTrip, Sanjeev Bikhchandani of Naukri and Deepinder Goyal of Zomato. It's now time to look at the views of an investor as well. And for this, I couldn't think of a better person than my close friend, Sushanto Mitra. A person who founded among the first and perhaps the most successful incubator in India, SINE, at IIT Bombay. And later went on to create Lead Angels, one of the leading angel networks in the country. By the way, Lead Angels has invested in many of the start-ups that I have discussed in this book, namely GO DESi, Belita, PlanetSpark and Auntie Fung's. So, it'll be great to get his perspective on these companies. Let's hear him out:

Every investor looks for a DREAM Founder. That much should be obvious. But what does this entail? Well, first of all, you must have a dream. And you must be passionate about this dream. No half measures. You'll have lots of situations when the chips are down, such as the Covid pandemic. It is your passion that will get you through these tough times. As a classic example, look at PlanetSpark and Auntie Fung's, both of which Dhruv has spoken about. In both these cases, the businesses had to shut down, and it was passion and determination that led to the founders pivoting and becoming successful once again. Incidentally, that was one major reason for Lead Angels to invest in these two companies— the passion we saw in the founders.

And then of course, you need to stand out in a crowd. Be confident, be assertive, and you'll find people flocking to you— whether it is team members, customers or investors. You must remember, as investors, we have thousands of hopeful founders approaching us for funding. You've got to stand out in the crowd to get our attention—and ultimately our money. And, by the way, passion and confidence go together.

Of course, you've got to be persuasive as well. You must be able and willing to sell your idea to others—whether it is your team members, customers, investors, or just about anyone else. Remember the story of GO DESi and what Vinay Kothari did when Covid hit the country? He needed to get permission from multiple local authorities in Karnataka, and that needed loads and loads of persuasion. Which is exactly what he managed.

Finally, you may have all these qualities, but there is one last thing you must have—humility. The ability and willingness to accept that you could be wrong. What Dhruv calls 'responsibility'. The willingness to take advice from others. After all, there are lots of people out there who could be smarter than you. Be willing to listen to them and learn from them

With that, let me wish you all the best in your venture. And whenever you are looking for funding, I would be happy to meet you!

Thanks a lot, Sushanto. I'm sure many of the young DREAM Founders reading this book would be delighted to take you up on your offer.

Section VI

Before You Leave . . .

28

Just in Case You've Forgotten

My friend, that brings me to the end of all the gyan I wanted to share with you. There is more, of course, but that will have to wait for another book. Now, if you haven't slept through the book, you would realize that there is a fair amount of advice that I've shared, based on my learning from all the founders that I have had the privilege of meeting. And by now, you probably have advice pouring out of your ears. But remember, all this is simply advice. What you do with it is entirely up to you.

Before I leave you, I thought I'd summarize what I've said right through the book. Just in case you've forgotten.

First of all, make sure you have a DREAM. And that too, a big dream. One that you are really, really passionate about. That's the starting point. And, of course, you must have the PERFECT ATTITUDE to chase this dream.

Once you have these two in place, you are all set for action. Where you build the RIGHT TEAM, and get into EXECUTION mode. Which of these comes first? Well, they are likely to take place more or less in parallel. For instance, if you are planning to take on a co-founder or two, it's good to get them in place right in the beginning. And, of course, as you start BUILDING your PRODUCT and planning out OPERATIONS, you'll keep

231

adding to this team. Till finally, you are all set to take your product or service to market.

Please do evaluate your business using the PERSISTENT framework I have shared. In my experience, successful start-ups tend to fit into this framework, whereas failures miss out on one or more parameters. And somewhere along the line, of course, you will put all this together in the form of a BUSINESS PLAN.

Yes, at some stage you might need funding, for which you would approach angel investors or later, VCs. What will they look at? You as the DREAM Founder and your PERSISTENT business model, of course.

I do hope you do not face any major crisis along your journey. But if you do, just grab it, and MAKE an OPPORTUNITY out of the CRISIS. That's what a true DREAM Founder would do.

Finally, there is one more thing that I wanted to share with you. In this book, you've heard many of the hugely successful founders in the world of start-ups. Guys like Deep Kalra of MakeMyTrip, Sanjeev Bikhchandani of Naukri, Deepinder Goyal of Zomato, Annurag Batra of *BW Businessworld*, Meena Ganesh of Portea Medical and Sushanto Mitra of Lead Angels. Have you noticed how most of them have similar views when it comes to DREAM Founders? And have you noticed that my views in this book have been similar as well? Have a big dream, focus on execution, ensure that you are flexible, build trust, etc. That's completely logical, isn't it? There are just a few key guidelines to becoming a successful founder. And everyone will give you the same guidelines. All you need to do is follow them!

Finally, dear founder, I'd love to see you succeed. And I do hope this book has at least a bit of a role in your success. Either way, do get back to me and share your feedback. I'm available on LinkedIn at www.linkedin.com/in/dhruvnathprof, and on email at dhruvn55@gmail.com. And I'd be delighted to hear from you.

And, who knows—you might end up with a lead role in my next book!

How This Book Was Really Written

So, you've met lots of founders. Some of whom built successful start-ups, whereas others failed. And, from time to time, you've also met their mentor, the bearded professor and angel investor.

One day, to celebrate and share this learning with each other, all these founders gathered together at a café—Akela, Mehringez, Harry, AK47, Hathi, Sattu and all the rest of them. Along with the bearded professor, of course. They chatted away happily about how much they had learnt from each other. And how this learning had helped each of them build their start-up.

Suddenly, one of them had an idea—I think it was Hathi, but I'm not sure. He turned to the professor and said, 'Sir, we have learnt so much from you and from each other, about building successful start-ups. But there are lakhs of other founders out there who can benefit from all this learning. Sir, why don't you write a book on this subject, where you put down all our stories?'

As if on cue, the others joined in the chorus. 'Yes sir. Brilliant idea. That way, many more founders like us can benefit from these experiences.'

The professor took a sip of his coffee and thought for a moment. And then he took another sip and thought some more. And more. But if you had been there, you would have noticed that he was smiling. As he ordered one final cup of coffee, a close observer could see that he was grinning from ear to ear. 'That's a great idea. Yes, I think I will!'

And with that, Professor Dhruv Nath put down all these stories and the learning in the form of a book.

And that, my friend, is the book you are holding!

Acknowledgements

Now that you've read this book, I must share something with you. Yes, I'm the author of the book. After all, it *does* have my name on the cover. And the royalty I get out of it *does* go into my bank account. But what about the material? All the stories and cases and successes and failures? All that gyan? Where has that come from?

Aha. That gyan, my friend, comes from those hundreds of young founders out there, who I've had the privilege of meeting over the past many, many years. Usually over coffee and pastries. Or sometimes, a more frugal fare of chai and samosas. And of course, over Zoom during Covid times. Yes, I might have been a mentor to them, but I have learnt far, far more from them than they have from me. That's where I got the masala for this book. And that's why I must thank all of them!

Next, among the people I have learnt a lot from, there are two who stand out. Two stalwarts of the start-up world, namely, Deep Kalra of MakeMyTrip and Sanjeev Bikhchandani of Naukri.com. Over the years, I have learnt so, so much from both of them. They have been kind enough to share their views in this book, and I'm sure you will learn a huge amount from them, as well.

My young friends, Deepinder Goyal of Zomato, Annurag Batra of *BW Businessworld* and Meena Ganesh of Portea Medical, have all contributed their wonderful knowhow and experience to this book. And of course, my close friend and co-author, Sushanto

Mitra, founder and CEO of Lead Angels, who has been my mentor in the area of start-up funding.

And then my even younger friends (and sometimes past students), Puneet Goyal and Rohit Prakash of iDream, Akash Gehani of Instamojo, Vinay Kothari of Go DESi, Garima and Akshay Jain of Belita, Subhradeep Bhowmik and Satrajit Das of Aunty Fung's, Shrey Sardana and Nitin Goyal of Grest, and Maneesh Dhooper and Kunal Malik of PlanetSpark. All of whom I have pestered, and then pestered some more, to worm out details of their great start-ups. Whose stories I have told you in these pages.

Penguin Random House India has been a great publisher, starting with my wonderful young friend and editor, Radhika Marwah. And of course, Vijesh Kumar, Ralph Rebello, Sameer Mahale, Anuj Sharma, Gopal Kabta and Saleheen Mohammed. Along with all the other 'Penguinites' who I've never met, but who worked brilliantly behind the scenes to get this book to the shape it finally took.

My children, Malvika and Siddharth, deserve a special mention for putting up with a peculiar father, who goes into long spells of hibernation to write some silly books. In spite of which, they have supported me through and through. Along with the children who joined the family later (or maybe I should call them young adults)—Niraj and Deeksha. And of course, baby Shloka—the one who calls me Nana. Yes, I must thank all my five children— for being there with me. And my parents, who have encouraged me in whatever I wanted to do, ever since I was born—or more correctly, since the age of two, when I was able to communicate my thoughts somewhat coherently.

Now if you've seen movies (I'm sure you have), you would know that the most important person is mentioned last of all— the Director. The one who is not seen on the screen, but has a key hand in everything that is done. That is Rajni—the only girlfriend I've ever had—and who I married several years ago. It is not easy to manage a home and family and kids almost single-handedly, when your husband has got it into his head to write what he fondly imagines are great books. But she has come out of this with flying colours. (By the way, I hope she reads this part!)

I hope I haven't missed anyone. But even if I have, I believe I have given you enough names. To blame, just in case you don't like the book!